Pocket Rough Guide

MADRID

written and researched by

SIMON BASKETT

D0206383

MAR   2016

Contents

<< CATÉDRAL DE LA ALMUDENA AND PALACIO REAL
< CUPOLA OF SAN FRANCISCO EL GRANDE

INTRODUCTION TO

MADRID

The sunniest, highest and liveliest capital city in Europe, Madrid has a lot to take pride in. Indeed, its inhabitants, the *Madrileños*, are so proud of their city that they modestly declare "desde Madrid al Cielo": that after Madrid there is only one remaining destination – Heaven. While their claim may be open to dispute, this compact, frenetic and fascinating city certainly has bags of appeal and its range of attractions has made it a deservedly popular short-break destination.

PALACIO REAL

Best places for tapas

There is a vast array of bars in Madrid, serving up tasty tapas: take a stroll around Huertas, La Latina, Chueca and Malasaña and you will stumble on some of the best. A few of our favourites are: *Los Gatos* (p.63), *La Chata* (p.36), *El Tempranillo* (p.37), *Cervecería Cervantes* (p.78), *La Toscana* (p.63), *Casa del Abuelo* (p.62) and *El Bocaito* (p.88).

King Felipe II plucked Madrid from provincial oblivion when he made it capital of the Spanish empire in 1561. The former garrison town enjoyed an initial Golden Age when literature and the arts flourished, but centuries of decline and political turmoil followed. However, with the death of the dictator Franco in 1975 and the return to democracy the city had a second burst of creativity, *La Movida Madrileña*, an outpouring of hedonistic, highly innovative and creative forces embodied by film director Pedro Almodóvar. In recent years Madrid has undergone a major facelift, with the completion of state-of-the-art extensions to the leading museums, the redevelopment of the river area and the regeneration of some of the historic parts of the centre.

The vast majority of the millions of visitors make a beeline for the Prado, the Reina Sofía and the Thyssen-Bornemisza, three magnificent galleries that give the city a weighty claim to

being the "European capital of art". Of equal appeal to football fans is the presence of one of the world's most glamorous and successful clubs, Real Madrid. Aside from these heavy hitters, there's also a host of smaller museums, palaces and parks, not to mention some of the best tapas, bars and nightlife in Spain.

FLAMENCO

When to visit

Traditionally, Madrid has a typical **continental climate**, cold and dry in winter, and hot and dry in summer. There are usually two rainy periods, in October/November and any time from late March to early May. With temperatures soaring to over 40ºC in July and August, the best times to visit are generally **spring** and **autumn**, when the city is pleasantly warm. The short, sharp winter takes many visitors by surprise, but crisp, sunny days with clear blue skies compensate for the drop in temperature.

Although Madrid is increasingly falling into line with other European capitals, many places still shut down in **August** as its inhabitants head for the coast or countryside. Luckily for visitors, and those *Madrileños* who choose to remain, sights and museums remain open and nightlife takes on a momentum of its own.

Madrid's short but eventful history has left behind a mosaic of traditions, cultures and cuisines, and you soon realize it's the inhabitants who play a big part in the city's appeal. Despite the morale-sapping economic crisis, *Madrileños* still retain an almost insatiable appetite for enjoying themselves, whether it be hanging out in the cafés or on the summer terrazas, packing the lanes of the Rastro flea market, filling the restaurants or playing hard and late in the bars and clubs. The nightlife for which Madrid is renowned is merely an extension of the Madrileño character and the capital's inhabitants consider other European cities positively dull by comparison with their own. The city centre is a mix of bustling, labyrinthine streets and peaceful squares, punctuated by historic architectural reminders of the past. As with many of its international counterparts, an influx of fast-food franchises and chain stores has challenged the once dominant local bars and shops, but in making the transition from provincial backwater to major European capital, Madrid has managed to preserve many key elements of its own stylish and quirky identity.

RETIRO PARK

MADRID AT A GLANCE

>> EATING

Eating out in Madrid is one of the highlights of any visit to the city. There's plenty to suit every pocket, from budget backstreet bars to high-class designer restaurants, and a bewildering range of cuisines encompassing tapas, traditional Madrileño and Spanish regional dishes. Lunch is taken late, with few *Madrileños* starting before 2pm, while dinner begins around 9pm. Opening hours can be flexible, with many bars and restaurants closing on Sunday evenings or Monday and for all or part of August. You should spend at least one evening sampling the tapas bars around Santa Ana/Huertas and La Latina. Chueca and Malasaña have some superb traditional bars and bright new restaurants, serving some of the most creative food in the city. The smarter district of Salamanca contains few bars of note, but some extremely good (and expensive) restaurants.

>> DRINKING

Madrid is packed with a variety of bars, cafés and terrazas. In fact, they are a central feature of Madrileño life and hanging out in bars is one of the best, and most pleasant, ways to get the feel of the city and its people. The areas bordering Puerta del Sol, in and around Cava Baja and Plaza Chueca are some of the liveliest, but you can stumble across a great bar in almost every street in the city centre.

>> NIGHTLIFE

As you'd expect with a city whose inhabitants are known as the "gatos" (the cats), there's a huge variety of nightlife on offer in the Spanish capital. The mainstays of the Madrid scene are the *bares de copas*, which get going around 11pm and stay open till 2am. The flashier *discotecas* are rarely worth investigating until around 1 or 2am, although queues often build up quickly after this time. Alonso Martínez, Argüelles and Moncloa are student hangouts, Salamanca is for the wealthy and chic, while head for Malasaña and Chueca if you want to be at the cutting edge of trendiness. You'll find a more eclectic mix on offer in the streets around Sol and Santa Ana.

>> SHOPPING

Head for Gran Vía and Calle Preciados if you're looking for department and chain stores and for the streets around Plaza Mayor if you're on the hunt for traditional establishments. For fashion and designer labels, the smartest addresses are in Salamanca, but more alternative designers are in Malasaña and Chueca. Fans of street fashion will like the shops on C/Fuencarral. Most areas of the city have their own *mercados* (indoor food markets), many of which have been given a makeover, but for the classic Madrileño shopping experience make your way to the flea market in the Rastro on a Sunday.

OUR RECOMMENDATIONS FOR WHERE TO EAT, DRINK AND SHOP ARE LISTED AT THE END OF EACH CHAPTER.

Day One in Madrid

1 The Prado > pp.66–67. The Prado contains a fabulous array of masterpieces by artistic greats such as Bosch, El Greco, Titian, Rubens Velázquez and Goya.

2 The Retiro > p.72. Ward off any museum fatigue by freshening up with a stroll around beautiful Retiro park.

🍴 **Lunch** > p.50. For a taste of some classic Castillian cuisine, try the well-regarded *Asador Arizmendi* in Tirso de Molina.

3 The Palacio Real > pp.38–39. Marvel at the magnificent, over-the-top decor in this one-time royal residence now used only for ceremonial purposes.

☕ **Coffee** > p.44. Looking out over the plaza towards the royal palace, the elegant *Café de Oriente* makes a great place for a relaxing drink.

4 Plaza Mayor > p.28. Built when the city became Spain's capital in the sixteenth century, Madrid's atmospheric main square retains an aura of traditional elegance.

5 Madrid de los Austrias > p.28. Take a step back in time and explore the twisting streets of ancient Madrid around La Latina.

🍴 **Dinner** > pp.62–63. Hit the tapas trail around Huertas. Hop from bar to bar, sampling local specialities. *Casa Alberto*, *Casa González* and *Casa del Abuelo II* are good places to make a start.

6 Flamenco > p.51. Finish the night off with some authentic flamenco at *Casa Patas*.

Day Two in Madrid

1 The Thyssen >
p.72. An outstanding art
collection assembled by the
Thyssen-Bornemisza dynasty and
providing an unprecedented excursion
through Western art.

2 The Santiago Bernabéu > p.93.
Home to the all-star Real Madrid, a
tour of this awesome stadium is a
must for any football fan. Better still,
take in a game.

Lunch > p.88. Prepare
yourself for a spot of
shopping in Chueca and Malasaña by
sampling a mouth-watering range of
tapas at *El Bocaito*.

3 Shopping > p.85. Chueca and
Malasaña are home to some of the
city's hippest fashion outlets and most
interesting independent stores.

4 Museo Reina Sofía > p.70.
An impressive home for Spain's
collection of contemporary art,
worth the visit if only to see
Picasso's *Guernica*.

5 Gourmet Experience > p.88.
Take in some of the best views in
Madrid from the terrace bars on
the ninth floor of El Corte Inglés
in Callao.

Dinner > p.34. *El Botin* is
reputedly the oldest *meson*
in the city and serves up superb,
traditional Castillian food.

6 Club > p.45. Work off some
calories with a dance at one of
Madrid's clubs. *Joy Madrid* has
an eclectic mix of music, a fun
atmosphere and a fantastic setting for
a late-night drink.

Budget Madrid

Many of Madrid's biggest sights are free at certain times of the week, while others charge no entry fee at all. Here are some suggestions on how to spend a great day without spending a penny on anything, apart from food and drink.

1 Museo de San Isidro > p.33. Housed in a sixteenth-century mansion that was supposedly once home to the city's patron saint, this museum traces the early history of the Spanish capital.

2 Museo de Historia de Madrid > p.84. Now fully reopened after a lengthy refurbishment, you can get a rundown of the history of the city at this free museum.

Lunch > p.50. With a great three-course set lunch menu at around €11, *La Sanabresa* is one of the best-value local restaurants in the city.

4 Templo de Debod > p.102. Shipped stone by stone from the banks of the River Nile, this ancient Egyptian temple is an incongruous sight in the city. The little exhibition inside is free.

5 The Prado > p.66. Head here between 6 and 8pm on weekdays (Sun 5–7pm) and you'll see an unparalleled collection of art for nothing.

6 The Retiro > p.72. Take a stroll by the lake in the Retiro park to relax and unwind.

Dinner > p.106. The cheap and cheerful *Casa Mingo* serves some fantastic roast chicken and bottled cider.

3 Palacio Real > p.38. Visit the sumptuous palace on a Wednesday or Thursday afternoon and you'll get in for nothing – be prepared to queue.

7 Río Manzanares > Finish off the evening with a stroll by the redeveloped river area by the Puente de Segovia.

Off-the-beaten-track Madrid

If you've got the time and have done the big sights, then why not take a break from the crowds and seek out some of Madrid's lesser-known, but highly rewarding attractions. Here are some of our suggestions.

1 Monasterio de las Descalzas Reales > p.42. Hidden behind an innocuous-looking door, this sixteenth-century convent is brimming full of artistic treasures.

2 San Francisco el Grande > p.33. Limited opening hours mean that this magnificent church and its frescoes are often overlooked.

3 Campo del Moro > p.41. Surprisingly under-visited, this English-style park below the Palacio Real provides a verdant retreat away from the bustle of the nearby streets.

4 Museo de Cerralbo > p.99. A charming museum housed in a beautifully restored mansion, home to the eclectic treasures of the nineteenth-century aristocrat, the Marqués de Cerralbo.

Lunch > p.78. Tucked away at the bottom of one of the little streets in Huertas, *La Verónica* serves an excellent *menú del dia*.

5 Museo Nacional del Romanticismo > p.84. This delightful museum recreates bourgeois life in nineteenth-century Madrid.

6 Museo Sorolla > p.91. The artist's elegant former home provides the perfect setting for his luminescent paintings.

7 Museo Lázaro Galdiano > p.93. Well off the tourist trail, this former private collection gets less than its fair share of attention and yet it houses an amazing cornucopia of art treasures.

Drink > p.99. Try out the little-known Plaza de Comendadoras and its terrazas for a pre-meal *aperitivo*.

Dinner > p.107. Try out some delicious home cooking at the popular *Gabriel* restaurant on Calle Conde Duque.

11

Big sights

1 Museo del Prado Quite simply one of the greatest art museums in the world. > **p.66**

2 **Museo Thyssen-Bornemisza** A superb collection of art put together by the Thyssen family and acting as a marvellous complement to the Prado. **> p.72**

4 **Estadio Santiago Bernabéu** The Galácticos may have gone, but this magnificent stadium merits a visit even if you are unable to get to a game. **> p.93**

3 **Palacio Real** A sumptuous royal palace reflecting the past glories of the Spanish royal family. **> p.38**

5 **Museo Reina Sofía** An essential stop on the art circuit, the Reina Sofía is home to Picasso's iconic masterpiece *Guernica*. **> p.70**

Eating out

1 Regional dishes Madrid offers every regional style of Spanish cooking. Try *La Barraca* for an authentic Valencian paella. **> p.86**

2 Haute cuisine David Muñoz's Michelin-starred *DiverXO* is currently one of Madrid's most highly regarded restaurants. **> p.96**

3 Tapas For an authentic night out eating tapas, copy the locals and go bar-hopping in Huertas or La Latina. **> p.62 & p.36**

4 Eating alfresco When you start to feel the heat, head outside to eat. The summer rooftop terrace at *Gau Café* has great views. **> p.50**

5 Madrid specialities The meat and chickpea stew *cocido* is one of the city's traditional dishes – try it out at *Malacatín*. **> p.50**

After dark

1 Bar culture Bars are a central feature of Madrileño life. The *Taberna Ángel Sierra* on Plaza Chueca is a classic choice. > **p.89**

3 Cocktails Start or finish a Madrid night out with some cocktails. The stylish *Del Diego* serves up some of the best in town. **> p.89**

2 Flamenco Andalucía may be the home of flamenco, but Madrid has some top acts. *Casa Patas* is a favourite. **> p.51**

4 Clubbing Madrid has a massive range of clubs, from unpretentious *bares de copas* to serious cutting-edge dance venues. **> p.7**

5 Terrazas As temperatures soar, life moves outside and so do the bars – head for the terrazas in Plaza Santa Ana or La Latina. **> p.63 & p.37**

Museums and galleries

1 **Real Fábrica de Tapices** A fascinating museum and a thriving workshop, allowing visitors the chance to view works in progress. > **p.76**

3 Museo Sorolla The life and works of artist Joaquín Sorolla is housed in his lovely former residence. > **p.91**

2 Museo Arqueológico Nacional An impressive collection of Visigothic, Roman, Greek and Egyptian finds in a beautiful refurbished building next to Plaza Colón. > **p.91**

5 Museo Lázaro Galdiano A treasure-trove of paintings, furniture and *objets d'art* in this personal collection assembled by publisher and businessman José Lázaro Galdiano. > **p.93**

4 Real Academia de Bellas Artes It may not boast the heavyweight attractions of the big three, but this gallery contains some captivating work by Goya, El Greco, José de Ribera and Zurbarán. > **p.56**

Green spaces

1 Casa de Campo Once part of the royal hunting estate, Casa de Campo is the biggest and wildest of the city's parks. > **p.103**

2 The Retiro This city-centre park has become *Madrileños'* favourite playground, with a boating lake and a crystal palace hosting regular exhibitions. **> p.72**

3 Campo del Moro One of the city's most beautiful, and underused, parks with shady paths and ornamental pools. **> p.41**

5 Parque del Oeste The lovely Parque del Oeste contains assorted statues, a fragrant rose garden and even a genuine Egyptian temple. **> p.102**

4 Jardínes Botánicos Dating back to the eighteenth century, the botanical gardens form an amazingly tranquil oasis in the city. **> p.73**

Kids

1 Parque de Atracciones A popular theme park situated in Casa de Campo with a vast range of rides catering for all ages. > **p.104**

3 The Retiro The Retiro park has plenty of child-friendly attractions including play areas, puppet shows, duck ponds and a boating lake. > **p.72**

2 The Teleférico For a bird's-eye view of the city, take the cable car across the Manzanares river to Casa de Campo. > **p.103**

4 Madrid's Zoo Casa de Campo is home to an attractive zoo complete with lions, bears, koalas, pandas, sharks and many reptiles. > **p.104**

5 Museo de Ferrocarril With its model railways and array of full-size locomotives, this museum will be a hit with most children and many parents too. > **p.49**

Madrid de los Austrias

Named after the royal family and their original homeland, the district known as Madrid de los Austrias, or Habsburg Madrid, is made up of some of the oldest and most atmospheric parts of the city. Centred around extravagant Plaza Mayor, the area is a twisting grid of streets, filled with Flemish-inspired architecture of red brick and grey stone. Most visitors only make it to the Plaza Mayor and its over-priced cafés and restaurants, but there are appealing sights scattered throughout the area, especially in the *barrio* (district) of La Latina, which stretches south of the square. This region is also home to some of the city's best restaurants, tapas bars and flamenco tablaos, especially around calles Almendro, Cava Baja and Cava Alta.

PLAZA MAYOR

Ⓜ **Sol.** MAP PP.30–31, POCKET MAP C12

The splendidly theatrical Plaza Mayor was originally the brainchild of Felipe II who, in the late sixteenth century, wished to construct a more prestigious focus for his new capital. The Casa de la Panadería on the north side of the square is the oldest building, dating from 1590, but, like much of the plaza, it was rebuilt after fires in the seventeenth and eighteenth centuries. The gaudy frescoes that adorn the facade were only added in 1992. It now houses the municipal tourist office (daily 9.30am–8.30pm).

Capable of holding up to fifty thousand people, the square was used for state occasions, *autos-de-fé* (public trials of heretics followed, usually, by burning of the victims), plays and bullfights. The large bronze equestrian statue in the middle is of Felipe III and dates from 1616.

BUILDINGS NEAR PLAZA MAYOR

Today, Plaza Mayor is primarily a tourist haunt, full of expensive outdoor cafés and restaurants. However, an air of grandeur clings to the plaza and it still hosts public functions, from outdoor theatre and music to Christmas fairs and a Sunday stamp and coin market.

CALLE MAYOR

Ⓜ Sol. MAP PP.30–31, POCKET MAP A12–D12

One of the oldest thoroughfares in the city, Calle Mayor was for centuries the route for religious processions from the Palacio Real to the Monastery of Los Jerónimos. The street is now home to souvenir shops and bars and is flanked by the facades of some of the most evocative buildings in the city. Set back from the road, near the entrance to the Plaza Mayor, is the splendid decorative ironwork of the **Mercado de San Miguel** (Sun–Wed 10am–midnight, Thurs–Sat 10am–2am; Ⓦ www .mercadodesanmiguel.es; see p.36). Built in 1916, it was formerly one of the old-style food markets scattered throughout the city, but it has now been refurbished and converted into a stylish tourist-oriented emporium complete with oyster and champagne bar.

SAN NICOLÁS DE LOS SERVITAS

Plaza de San Nicolás 1 Ⓜ Ópera. Tues–Sat 8.30–9.30am & 6.30–8.30pm, Sun & hols 10am–1.45pm & 6.30–8.45pm. MAP PP.30–31, POCKET MAP A12

Largely rebuilt between the fifteenth and seventeenth centuries, Madrid's oldest church still includes a twelfth-century Mudéjar tower featuring traditional Arabic horseshoe arches. Juan de Herrera, architect of El Escorial (see p.116), is buried in the crypt.

STATUE OF ÁLVARO DE BAZÁN, PLAZA DE LA VILLA

PLAZA DE LA VILLA

Ⓜ Sol. MAP PP.30–31, POCKET MAP A12

This charming plaza, just off Calle Mayor, showcases three centuries of Spanish architectural development. The oldest buildings are the simple but eye-catching fifteenth-century **Torre y Casa de Los Lujanes**, where Francis I of France is said to have been imprisoned by Emperor Charles V after the Battle of Pavia in 1525. On the south side of the square is the **Casa de Cisneros**, constructed for the nephew of Cardinal Cisneros (early sixteenth-century Inquisitor-General and Regent of Spain) in the intricate Plateresque style.

The **Casa de la Villa** occupies the remaining side. An emblem of Habsburg Madrid, it was constructed in fits and starts from the mid-seventeenth century to house the offices and records of the council, who recently moved on to more grandiloquent headquarters in the Palacio de Cibeles. The initial design by Juan Gómez de Mora wasn't completed until 1693, 45 years after his death, and was mellowed by the addition of Baroque details in the eighteenth century.

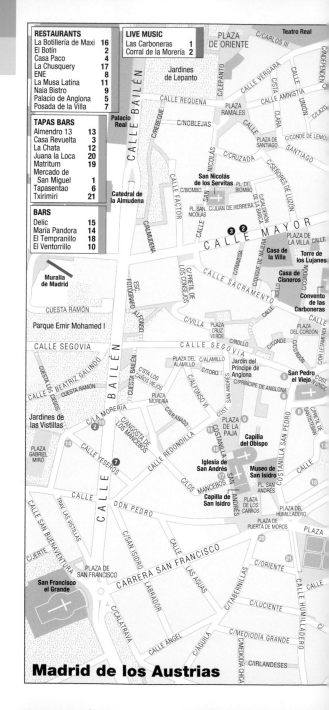

Madrid de los Austrias

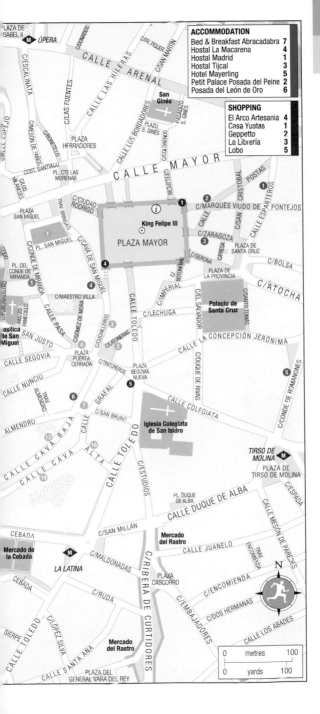

ACCOMMODATION

Bed & Breakfast Abracadabra	7
Hostal La Macarena	4
Hostal Madrid	1
Hostal Tijcal	3
Hotel Mayerling	5
Petit Palace Posada del Peine	2
Posada del León de Oro	6

SHOPPING

El Arco Artesanía	4
Casa Yustas	1
Geppetto	2
La Librería	3
Lobo	5

PARQUE EMIR MOHAMED I

🚇 **Ópera.** MAP PP.30–31, POCKET MAP B6

It is easy to miss this small, enclosed park opposite the crypt, but it is notable for the fragments of the city walls that date back to the ninth and twelfth centuries. The park lies on the Cuesta de la Vega, former site of one of the main entrances to Muslim Madrid, while nearby, the narrow, labyrinthine streets of the former Moorish quarter, La Morería, are still clearly laid out on medieval lines.

CONVENTO DE LAS CARBONERAS

Plaza Conde de Miranda 3 🚇 **Sol.** MAP PP.30–31, POCKET MAP B13

Founded in the early seventeenth century, this convent belongs to the closed Hieronymite Order. It's famous for its home-made biscuits and cakes – a tradition in Spanish convents since the time of St Teresa of Ávila, who gave out sweetened egg yolks to the poor – which can be purchased every day (9.30am–1pm & 4–6.30pm). Ring the bell above the sign reading *venta de dulces* to be let in, then follow the signs to the *torno*; the business takes place by means of a revolving drum to preserve the closed nature of the order.

BASÍLICA DE SAN MIGUEL

C/San Justo 4 🚇 **La Latina** or Sol. July to mid-Sept Mon–Sat 10am–1.15pm & 6–9.15pm, Sun 9.45am–1.30pm & 6.30–9.15pm; mid-Sept to June Mon–Sat 9.45am–1.30pm & 5.30–9pm, Sun 9.45am–2.15pm & 6–9.15pm. MAP PP.30–31, POCKET MAP B13

Standing among a host of other graceful buildings – most of which house local government offices – San Miguel stands out as one of the few examples of a full-blown Baroque church in Madrid. Designed at the end of the seventeenth century for Don Luis, the precocious 5-year-old Archbishop of Toledo and youngest son of Felipe V, its features include an unconventional convex facade with four recesses, each containing a statue, variously representing Charity, Strength, Faith and Hope.

SAN PEDRO EL VIEJO

Costanilla de San Pedro 🚇 **La Latina.** Mon–Sat 9am–12.30pm & 5–8pm. MAP PP.30–31, POCKET MAP B13

At the heart of busy La Latina is the Mudéjar tower of San Pedro El Viejo. The second-oldest church in Madrid, it's said to have been founded in the fourteenth century by Alfonso XI, and stands on the site of an old mosque, though most of the church was rebuilt in the seventeenth century.

PLAZA DE LA PAJA

🚇 **La Latina.** MAP PP.30–31, POCKET MAP A14

One of the real gems of old Madrid, this ancient sloping plaza was the commercial and civic hub of the city before the construction of the Plaza Mayor, and was once surrounded by a series of mansions owned by local dignitaries. With the restored houses beaming down on the former market square, this is a rare peaceful and traffic-free spot in the city. At the bottom is the pretty little Jardín del

PLAZA DE LA PAJA

Príncipe de Anglona (daily: winter 10am–6pm; summer 10am–10pm), a survivor of the gardens that used to be attached to the nearby mansions.

IGLESIA DE SAN ANDRÉS, CAPILLA DEL OBISPO AND CAPILLA DE SAN ISIDRO

Plaza de San Andrés Ⓜ La Latina. Mon–Thurs & Sat 8am–1pm & 6–8pm, Fri 6–8pm, Sun 10am–1pm. MAP PP.30–31, POCKET MAP A14

The Iglesia de San Andrés was badly damaged by an anarchist attack in 1936, and the adjoining Gothic Capilla del Obispo (guided tours Tues 10am–12.30pm & Thurs 4–5.30pm; reservation only on ☏ 915 592 874 or in the cathedral museum; €2), with its polychromed altarpiece and alabaster tombs, was only recently reopened following a forty-year restoration. The main church and the Baroque Capilla de San Isidro are reached by walking round the building into Plaza de San Andrés. The chapel was built in the mid-seventeenth century to hold the remains of Madrid's patron saint, San Isidro (since moved to the Iglesia de San Isidro), and the interior features a beautifully sculpted dome.

MUSEO DE SAN ISIDRO

Plaza de San Andrés 2 Ⓜ La Latina Ⓦ www .madrid.es/museosanisidro. Tues–Sun 9.30am–8pm; Aug until 2.30pm Tues–Fri. Free. MAP PP.30–31, POCKET MAP A14

Housed in a reconstructed sixteenth-century mansion – supposedly home to San Isidro – this museum includes an exhibition on the history of Madrid. The city's archeological collection is in the basement, while the rest of the building is given over to the saint himself, with displays relating to his life and miraculous activities. The house also contains a well, site

IGLESIA DE SAN ANDRÉS

of one of Isidro's most famous exploits: he rescued his young son from the murky depths, by praying until the waters rose to the surface. The seventeenth-century chapel contained within the museum is built on the spot where the saint was said to have died in 1172.

SAN FRANCISCO EL GRANDE

Plaza de San Francisco 11 Ⓜ La Latina. Tues–Sat 10.30am–1pm & 4–6.30pm (ticket office closes 6pm). €3 with guided tour. MAP PP.30–31, POCKET MAP B7

Following a twenty-year restoration programme, you can appreciate this magnificent eighteenth-century domed church in something close to its original glory. Inside, each of the six chapels is designed in a distinct style ranging from Mozarab and Renaissance to Baroque and Neoclassical. Look out for the early Goya, *The Sermon of San Bernadino of Siena*, in the chapel on your immediate left as you enter, which contains a self-portrait of the 37-year-old artist (in the yellow suit on the right).

Even if your Spanish is not that good, follow the guided tour to get a glimpse of the church's other art treasures, including paintings by José de Ribera and Zurbarán.

Shops

EL ARCO ARTESANIA

Plaza Mayor 9 Ⓜ Sol. Mon–Sat 11am–8pm, Sun 11am–2.30pm. MAP PP.30–31, POCKET MAP B13

Though at the heart of tourist Madrid, the goods for sale here are a far cry from the swords, lace and castanets that fill most shops in the area. Crafts include ceramics, leather, wood, jewellery and textiles.

CASA YUSTAS

Plaza Mayor 30 Ⓜ Sol Ⓦ casayustas.com. Mon–Sat 9.30am–9.30pm, Sun 11am–9.30pm. MAP PP.30–31, POCKET MAP C12

Established in 1886, Madrid's oldest hat shop sells every conceivable model from pith helmets and commando berets to panamas and bowlers. There's also a large range of souvenir-style goods, including Lladró porcelain figurines.

GEPPETTO

C/Mayor 78 Ⓜ Sol Ⓦ geppettoitalia.com. Daily 10am–8.30pm. MAP PP.30–31, POCKET MAP A12

Surrounded by a host of garish souvenir shops, this little place offers something quite different: handmade wooden toys and trinkets from Italy. Perfect if you're buying for a small child.

CASA YUSTAS

LA LIBRERÍA

C/Mayor 80 Ⓜ Sol Ⓦ edicioneslalibreria.es. Mon–Fri 10am–2pm & 4.30–7.30pm, Sat 11am–2pm. MAP PP.30–31, POCKET MAP A12

Tiny place full of books just about Madrid. Most are in Spanish, but many would serve as coffee-table souvenirs. Also good for old prints of the city.

LOBO

C/Toledo 30 Ⓜ La Latina Ⓦ calzadoslobo.com. Mon–Fri 9.45am–1.45pm & 4.30–8pm, Sat 9.45am–1.45pm. MAP PP.30–31, POCKET MAP C13

Great old-fashioned shoe shop, with anything from espadrilles to Menorcan sandals (€25) in every conceivable colour. Excellent for kids' shoes.

Restaurants

LA BOTILLERÍA DE MAXI

C/Cava Alta 4 Ⓜ La Latina ☎913 651 249, Ⓦ labotilleriademaxi.com. Tues–Sat 12.30–4pm & 8.30pm–12.30am, Sun 12.30–6pm. Closed two weeks in Aug. MAP PP.30–31, POCKET MAP B14

A mix of fine traditional staples and interesting new dishes. Specialities include the Madrid classic *callos* (tripe in tomato sauce) and *rabo de toro* (oxtail), but they also serve international dishes such as Greek salad and Moroccan kebabs. A €10 lunchtime menu is available.

EL BOTÍN

C/Cuchilleros 17 Ⓜ Sol ☎913 664 217, Ⓦ botin.es. Daily 1–4pm & 8pm–midnight. MAP PP.30–31, POCKET MAP C13

Established in 1725, the atmospheric *El Botín* is cited in the *Guinness Book of Records* as Europe's oldest restaurant. Favoured by Hemingway, it's inevitably a tourist haunt, but not such a bad one. Highlights are the Castilian roasts – especially *cochinillo* (suckling pig) and *cordero lechal* (lamb).

CASA PACO

Plaza Puerta Cerrada 11 Ⓜ La Latina ☎ 913 663 166. Mon–Sat 1.30–4pm & 8pm–midnight. Closed Aug. MAP PP.30–31, POCKET MAP B13

This classic, traditional *comedor*, with no-nonsense service, dishes out some of the best meat dishes in town. Specializes in sirloin steak (*solomillo*), and another delicious cut known as *cebón de buey*. About €35 a head.

LA CHUSQUERY

C/Mancebos 2 Ⓜ La Latina ☎ 910 703 215, Ⓦ la-chusquery.es. Tues–Sat 1.30–4pm & 8.30pm–midnight, Sun 1.30–4pm. MAP PP.30–31, POCKET MAP A14

New arrival on the La Latina scene, which serves up carefully selected dishes combining new Spanish cuisine and Asian influences. Specialities include Tataki butterfish, home-made *croquetas* and a delicious chocolate brownie dessert. Very reasonably priced (around €25 a head).

ENE

C/Nuncio 19 Ⓜ La Latina ☎ 913 662 591, Ⓦ enerestaurante.com. Mon–Wed, Thurs & Sun 1.30–4.30pm & 9pm–midnight, Fri & Sat until 1.30am. MAP PP.30–31, POCKET MAP A14

Fashionable bar/restaurant just below Plaza de la Paja serving a fusion-style €11 *menú del día* and a tasty but overpriced €22 brunch at weekends. Cocktails and DJs Thurs–Sun.

LA MUSA LATINA

Costanilla San Andrés 12 Ⓜ La Latina ☎ 913 540 255, Ⓦ grupolamusa.com. Mon–Wed 1pm–1am, Thurs 1pm–1.30am, Fri 1pm–2am, Sat 10am–2am, Sun 10am–1pm. MAP PP.30–31, POCKET MAP A14

Stylish place serving a great-value €11 *menú del día*, and a small selection of modern tapas such as vegetable tempura, fried green tomatoes and wok dishes. It has a cool brick-walled bar downstairs with DJ sessions.

POSADA DE LA VILLA

NAIA BISTRO

Plaza de la Paja 3 Ⓜ La Latina ☎ 913 662 783, Ⓦ naiabistro.com. Tues–Thurs 1.30–4.30pm & 8.30–11.30pm, Fri & Sat 1.30–5.30pm & 8.30pm–12.30am, Sun 1.30–5.30pm. MAP PP.30–31, POCKET MAP A14

Relaxed restaurant with light, airy decor serving up well presented creative cuisine in a fine setting on an ancient plaza. Starters include pumpkin ravioli with sage and gorgonzola; mains such as red tuna with citrus mayonnaise are also tempting. À la carte around €30 a head; group menus are also available.

PALACIO DE ANGLONA

C/Segovia 13 Ⓜ La Latina ☎ 913 653 153, Ⓦ palaciodeanglona.com. Tues–Sun 1.30–4pm & 8.30pm–2am. MAP PP.30–31, POCKET MAP A13

Housed in the cellars of an old mansion, this good-value restaurant has imaginative dishes (around €8–12 for mains) such as black spaghetti with prawns. Good cocktails in the bar too.

POSADA DE LA VILLA

C/Cava Baja 9 Ⓜ La Latina ☎ 913 661 860, Ⓦ posadadelavilla.com. Mon–Sat 1–4pm & 8pm–midnight, Sun 1–4pm. Closed Aug. MAP PP.30–31, POCKET MAP B14

La Latina's most attractive restaurant, spread over three floors of a seventeenth-century inn. Cooking is Madrileño, including superb roast lamb. Reckon on €50 per person.

LA CHATA

Tapas bars

ALMENDRO 13

C/Almendro 13 Ⓜ La Latina. Mon–Fri 1–4pm & 7.30pm–midnight, Sat, Sun & hols 1–5pm & 8pm–midnight. MAP PP.30-31, POCKET MAP B14

Packed at weekends, this fashionable wood-panelled bar serves great *fino* sherry and house specials of *huevos rotos* (fried eggs on a bed of crisps) and *roscas rellenas* (bread rings stuffed with various meats).

CASA REVUELTA

C/Latoneros 3 Ⓜ Sol or La Latina. Tues–Sat 1–4pm & 8pm–midnight, Sun 1–4pm. Closed Aug. MAP PP.30-31, POCKET MAP C13

A timeless, down-to-earth little bar located in an alleyway just south of Plaza Mayor. It serves a melt-in-the-mouth tapa of *bacalao frito* (battered cod).

LA CHATA

C/Cava Baja 24 Ⓜ La Latina Ⓦ lachatamadrid .net. Daily 1.30–4.30pm & 8.30pm–1am. Closed Tues & Wed lunchtime & Sun eve. MAP PP.30-31, POCKET MAP B14

One of the city's most traditional and popular tiled tapas bars, with hams hanging from the ceiling and taurine memorabilia

on the walls. Serves a good range of dishes, including excellent *rabo de toro* (oxtail) and *pimientos del piquillo rellenos* (stuffed onions and peppers).

JUANA LA LOCA

Plaza Puerta de Moros 4 Ⓜ La Latina Ⓦ juanalalocamadrid.com. Mon 8pm–midnight, Tues–Fri 1–5pm & 8pm–midnight, Sat & Sun 1pm–midnight or 1am. Closed Aug. MAP PP.30-31, POCKET MAP C7

Fashionable hangout serving inventive tapas – tortilla with caramelized onion, tuna carpaccio – and a great selection of very tasty, but fairly pricey, canapés.

MATRITUM

C/Cava Alta 17 Ⓜ La Latina Ⓦ matritum.es. Tues 8.30pm–midnight, Wed–Sun 1–4.30pm & 8.30pm–12.30am. Closed Aug. MAP PP.30-31, POCKET MAP B14

Delicious designer-style tapas, from stuffed sea urchin to grilled tuna with teriyaki vegetables. There's a collection of carefully selected wines too.

MERCADO DE SAN MIGUEL

Plaza de San Miguel Ⓜ Sol Ⓦ mercadodesan miguel.es. Sun–Wed 10am–midnight, Thurs–Sat 10am–2am. MAP PP.30-31, POCKET MAP B12

Transformed from a neighbourhood market into a hip location for an *aperitivo*, this beautiful wrought-iron *mercado* is worth exploring at almost any time of day. There's something for everyone, from vermouth and champagne to salt cod, oysters and sushi.

TAPASENTAO

C/Príncipe Anglona Ⓜ La Latina. Tues–Thurs 12.30pm–midnight, Fri–Sun 12.30pm–2am. Closed two weeks Aug. MAP PP.30-31, POCKET MAP A14

Just opposite the church of San Pedro el Viejo, this popular bar serves up a wide range of interesting and original tapas, many of which are suitable for vegetarians. Favourites include crunchy, fried aubergines, vegetable tempura and battered mushrooms.

TXIRIMIRI

C/Humilladero 6 ⓜ La Latina ⓦ txirimiri.es. Daily noon–midnight. MAP PP.30–31, POCKET MAP C7

Fantastic range of tapas and *pintxos* in this ever-popular bar beside the Mercado de la Cebada. Mouth-watering combinations include cuttlefish and langoustine risotto and their speciality, Unai hamburger.

Bars

DELIC

Costanilla San Andrés 14 ⓜ La Latina ⓦ delic.es. Tues–Sun 11am–2am. Closed first half of Aug. MAP PP.30–31, POCKET MAP A14

Serving home-made cakes, fruit juices and coffee, this is a pleasant café by day, transforming into a crowded but friendly cocktail bar by night.

MARÍA PANDORA

Plaza Gabriel Miró 1 ⓜ La Latina ⓦ maria pandora.com. Mon–Sat 7pm–2am, Sun 4pm–2am. Closed second half of Aug. MAP PP.30–31, POCKET MAP B7

An incongruous mix of *champagnería* (champagne bar) and library, where quality *cava* can be enjoyed with the perfect accompaniment of chocolates and mellow jazz.

EL TEMPRANILLO

C/Cava Baja 38 ⓜ La Latina. Daily 1–4pm & 8.30pm–midnight. Closed two weeks in Aug. MAP PP.30–31, POCKET MAP B14

Popular little wine bar serving a vast range of domestic wines by the glass. A great place to discover your favourite Spanish *vino* – and the tapas are excellent too.

EL VENTORRILLO

C/Bailén 14 ⓜ La Latina or Ópera. Daily 11am–1am, Fri & Sat till 2am. MAP PP.30–31, POCKET MAP C7

This popular *terraza* is great for a relaxing drink while enjoying the *vistillas* (little views) over the cathedral and mountains, but avoid the overpriced tapas.

Live music

LAS CARBONERAS

Plaza Conde de Miranda ⓜ Sol ☎ 915 428 677. ⓦ tablaolascarboneras.com. Mon–Sat: shows 8.30pm & 10.30pm; Fri & Sat also 11pm. MAP PP.30–31, POCKET MAP B13

Geared up for the tourist market, this *tablao* has gained a decent reputation on the flamenco scene with a good range of guest artists. At around €65 with dinner, it remains slightly cheaper than its rivals.

CORRAL DE LA MORERÍA

C/Morería 17 ⓜ La Latina or Ópera ☎ 913 658 446. ⓦ corraldelamoreria.com. Daily 7pm–2am; shows at 8.30pm & 10.30pm. MAP PP.30–31, POCKET MAP C7

An atmospheric, if expensive, venue for serious flamenco acts. Around €50 to see the show and double that if you want to dine in the restaurant as well.

CORRAL DE LA MORERÍA

Palacio Real and Ópera

Although the *barrio* only became fashionable in the mid-nineteenth century, the attractions found in the compact area around Ópera metro station date back as far as the 1500s. The imposing and suitably lavish Palacio Real (Royal Palace) dominates this part of the city, bordered by the somewhat disappointing Catedral de la Almudena and the tranquil gardens of the Campo del Moro. The restored Teatro Real and Plaza de Oriente bring some nineteenth-century sophistication to the area, while the two monastery complexes of la Encarnación and las Descalzas Reales conceal an astounding selection of artistic delights. For after-dark attractions, the area is home to one of the city's leading clubs as well as a handful of pleasant cafés and restaurants.

PALACIO REAL

C/Bailén Ⓜ Ópera or Sol Ⓦ patrimonio nacional.es. Daily: April–Sept 10am–8pm; Oct–March 10am–6pm; closed for state occasions and on Jan 1 & 6, May 1 & 15, Oct 12, Nov 9, Dec 24, 25 & 31. €11; free for EU citizens Mon–Thurs: Oct–March 4–6pm; April–Sept 6–8pm. MAP P.40, POCKET MAP B5–C5

The present Palacio Real (Royal Palace) was built by Felipe V after the ninth-century Arab-built Alcázar was destroyed by fire in 1734. The Bourbon monarch, who had been brought up in the more luxurious surroundings of Versailles, took the opportunity to replace it with an altogether grander affair. He did not, however, live to see its completion and the palace only became habitable in 1764 during the reign of Carlos III. Nowadays it's used only for ceremonial purposes, with the present royal family preferring the more modest Zarzuela Palace, 15km northwest of the city.

The ostentation lacking in the palace's exterior is more than compensated for inside, with swirling marble floors, celestial frescoes and gold furnishings. It's a flamboyant display of wealth and power that was firmly at odds with Spain's declining status at the time.

THE PALACIO REAL

CATEDRAL DE LA ALMUDENA

Look out for the grandiose **Salón del Trono** (Throne Room), the incredible oriental-style **Salón de Gasparini** (the Gasparini Room) and the marvellous **Sala de Porcelana** (Porcelain Room), decorated with one thousand gold, green and white interlocking pieces.

The palace outbuildings and annexes include the **Armería Real** (Royal Armoury), with its fascinating collection of guns, swords and armour. There's also a laboratory-like eighteenth-century **farmacia** (pharmacy) and a **Galería de Pinturas** which displays works by Caravaggio, Velázquez and Goya and also hosts temporary exhibitions.

JARDINES DE SABATINI

Ⓜ Ópera. Daily: April–Sept 9am–10pm; Oct–March 9am–9pm. MAP P.40, POCKET MAP B4–C4

The Jardines de Sabatini (Sabatini Gardens) make an ideal place from which to view the northern facade of the palace or to watch the sun go down. They contain a small ornamental lake, some fragrant magnolia trees and manicured hedges, while, in summer, they're often used as a concert venue.

CATEDRAL DE LA ALMUDENA

Ⓜ Ópera. Daily: 9am–8.30pm, July & Aug 10am–9pm. Not open for visits during Mass: Mon–Sat noon, 6pm & 7pm, Sun & hols 10.30am, noon, 1.30pm, 6pm & 7pm; July & Aug noon & 8pm. MAP P.40, POCKET MAP B6

Planned centuries ago, Madrid's cathedral, Nuestra Señora de la Almudena, was plagued by lack of funds, bombed in the Civil War and finally opened in 1993. More recently, it was the venue for the wedding of the then heir to the throne, Prince Felipe, and his former newsreader bride, Letizia Ortiz.

The cathedral's cold Gothic interior housed within its stark Neoclassical shell is not particularly inspiring, though the garish ceiling designs and the sixteenth-century altarpiece in the Almudena chapel are exceptions. To one side of the main facade is a small **museum** (Mon–Sat 10am–2.30pm; €6, €4 for Madrid residents, students and pensioners) containing some of the cathedral's treasures, though the main reason to visit is to gain access to the dome from where you can enjoy some fantastic views over the city. The entrance to the **crypt** (daily 10am–8pm) with its forest of columns and dimly lit chapels is on C/Mayor.

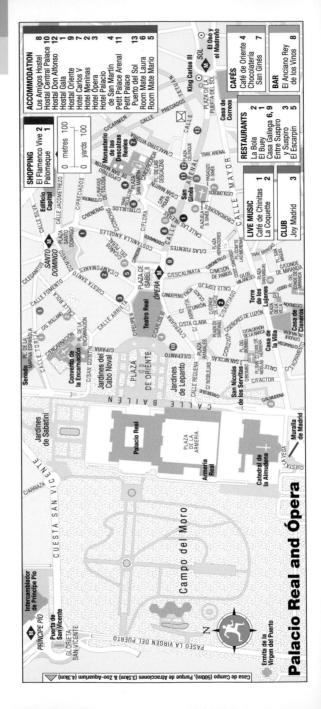

ACCOMMODATION
Los Amigos Hostel	8
Hostal Central Palace	10
Hostal Don Alfonso	12
Hostal Gala	1
Hostal Oriente	9
Hotel Carlos V	7
Hotel Meninas	2
Hotel Opera	3
Hotel Palacio de San Martín	4
Petit Palace Arenal	11
Petit Palace	
Puerta del Sol	13
Room Mate Laura	6
Room Mate Mario	5

SHOPPING
El Flamenco Vive	2
Palomeque	1

RESTAURANTS
La Bola	1
El Buey	2
Casa Gallega	6, 9
Entre Suspiro y Suspiro	3
El Escarpín	5

CAFÉS
Café de Oriente	4
Chocolatería San Ginés	7

BAR
El Anciano Rey de los Vinos	8
El Oso y el Madroño	

LIVE MUSIC
Café de Chinitas	1
La Coquette	2

CLUB
Joy Madrid	3

0 metres 100
0 yards 100

Palacio Real and Ópera

Casa de Campo (500m), Parque de Atracciones (3.5km) & Zoo-Aquarium (4.3km)

CAMPO DEL MORO

Entrance on Paseo de la Virgen del Puerto Ⓜ Príncipe Pío. Daily: April–Sept 10am–8pm; Oct–March 10am–6pm; closed occasionally for state occasions. MAP P.40, POCKET MAP A4–B6

One of the most underused – largely because of its inconvenient entrance down by the river – and beautiful of Madrid's parks, the Campo del Moro gets its name from being the site of the Moors' encampment, from where, in 1109, they mounted their unsuccessful attempt to reconquer Madrid. It later became a venue for medieval tournaments and celebrations. After the building of the Palacio Real several schemes to landscape the area were put forward, but it wasn't until 1842 that things got under way. Based around two monumental fountains, *Las Conchas* and *Los Tritones*, the grassy gardens are very English in style, featuring shady paths and ornamental pools, and provide an excellent refuge from the summer heat, as well as a splendid view of the palace.

PLAZA DE ORIENTE

Ⓜ Ópera. MAP P.40, POCKET MAP A11

The aristocratic, pedestrianized Plaza de Oriente is one of the most attractive open spaces in Madrid. The days when Franco used to address crowds here from the balcony of the royal palace now seem a distant memory, although a small number of neo-Fascists still gather here on the anniversary of his death, November 21.

The fountain in the centre was designed by Narciso Pascual y Colomer, who also transferred the bronze equestrian statue of Felipe IV here from the garden of the Buen Retiro Palace, near the Prado. Dating from 1640, this statue is reputedly the first-ever bronze featuring a rearing horse – Galileo is said to have helped with the calculations to make it balance. Other statues depict Spanish kings and queens, and were originally designed to adorn the palace facade, but were too heavy or, according to one version, too ugly, and were removed on the orders of Queen Isabel Farnese.

There's a very French feel to the buildings overlooking the square, with their glass-fronted balconies, underlined by the elegant neo-Baroque *Café de Oriente*, a favourite with the opera crowd.

PLAZA DE ORIENTE

TEATRO REAL

Plaza de Isabel II Ⓜ Ópera ☏ 915 160 660, ticket line ☏ 902 244 848, Ⓦ teatro-real.com. Open for visits daily 10.30am–1pm; closed mid-July to mid-Sept; reservations ☏ 915 160 696. €8; tickets on sale 9.15am–1pm at the box office. MAP P.40, POCKET MAP A11–B11

When it opened in 1850, the hulking grey hexagonal opera house became the hub of fashionable Madrid and staged highly successful works by Verdi and Wagner. It fell into decay in the late twentieth century and after a ten-year refurbishment – that should have lasted four – and a staggering US$150 million in costs, it finally reopened in October 1997. With its lavish red and gold decor, crystal chandeliers, state-of-the-art lighting and superb acoustics it makes a truly magnificent setting for opera, ballet and classical concerts. Tickets range from €10 to €400, but you'll need to book well in advance for the best seats.

CONVENTO DE LA ENCARNACIÓN

Plaza de la Encarnación 1 Ⓜ Ópera Ⓦ patrimonionacional.es. Tours only (some in English) Tues–Sat 10am–2pm & 4–6.30pm, Sun & hols 10am–3pm. €6; joint ticket with Monasterio de las Descalzas Reales €8, valid for 48 hours; Wed & Thurs 4–6.30pm free for EU citizens. MAP P.40, POCKET MAP A10

Founded in 1611 by Felipe III and his wife Margarita de Austria, this convent was intended as a retreat for titled women and merits a visit for its reliquary alone – one of the most important in the Catholic world. The solemn granite facade is the hallmark of architect Juan Gómez de Mora, also responsible for the Plaza Mayor. Much of the painting contained within is uninspiring, but there are some interesting items, including an extensive collection of royal portraits and a highly prized collection of sculptures of Christ. The library-like **reliquary** contains more than 1500 saintly relics from around the world: skulls, arms encased in beautifully ornate hand-shaped containers and bones from every conceivable part of the lot is a small glass bulb said to contain the blood of St Pantaleón – a fourth-century doctor martyr – which supposedly liquefies at midnight every July 26 (the eve of his feast day). Great tragedies are supposed to occur if the blood fails to liquefy. The tour ends with a visit to the Baroque-style church which features a beautifully frescoed ceiling and a marble-columned altarpiece.

MONASTERIO DE LAS DESCALZAS REALES

Plaza de las Descalzas 3 Ⓜ Callao, Sol or Ópera Ⓦ patrimonionacional.es. Tours only (some in English) Tues–Sat 10am–2pm & 4–6.30pm, Sun & hols 10am–3pm. €6; joint ticket with Convento de la Encarnación €8, valid for 48 hours; Wed & Thurs 4–6.30pm free for EU citizens. MAP P.40, POCKET MAP C10–C11

One of the less well-known treasures of Madrid, the "Monastery of the Barefoot Royal Ladies" was originally the site of a medieval palace. The building was transformed by Juana de Austria into a convent in 1564, and the architect of El Escorial, Juan Bautista de Toledo, was entrusted with its design. Juana was the youngest daughter of the Emperor Charles V and, at the age of 19, already the widow of Prince Don Juan of Portugal. Royal approval meant that it soon became home to a succession of titled ladies who brought with them an array of artistic treasures, helping the convent accumulate a fabulous collection

MONASTERIO DE LAS DESCALZAS REALES

of paintings, sculptures and tapestries. The place is still unbelievably opulent and remains in use as a religious institution, housing 23 shoeless nuns of the Franciscan order.

The magnificent main staircase connects a two-levelled cloister, lined with small but richly embellished chapels, while the Tapestry Room contains an outstanding collection of early seventeenth-century Flemish tapestries based on designs by Rubens. The other highlight of the tour is the Joyería (Treasury), piled high with jewels and relics of uncertain provenance. Royal portraits and beautiful, wooden sculptures, most of unknown origin, decorate other rooms.

SAN GINÉS

C/Arenal 13 Ⓜ Ópera/Sol. Daily 8.45am–1pm & 6–9pm. Free. MAP P.40, POCKET MAP C11

Of Mozarabic origin (built by Christians under Moorish rule), this ancient church was completely reconstructed in the seventeenth century. There is an El Greco canvas of the moneychangers being chased from the temple in the Capilla del Cristo (on show Mon 11.30am–1pm).

Shops

EL FLAMENCO VIVE

C/Conde de Lemos 7 Ⓜ Ópera or Sol Ⓦ el flamencovive.com. Mon–Sat 10.30am–2pm & 5–9pm. MAP P.40, POCKET MAP B12

A fascinating little slice of Andalucía in Madrid, specializing in all things flamenco, from guitars and CDs to dresses and books.

PALOMEQUE

C/Arenal 17 Ⓜ Ópera or Sol Ⓦ palomeque arte.com. Mon–Fri 9.30am–1.30pm & 4.30–8pm, Sat 9.30am–1.30pm. MAP P.40, POCKET MAP C11

Founded back in 1873, this somewhat incongrous religious superstore has kept its place amongst the fashion outlets, hotels and restaurants that line this busy shopping street. Inside you'll find all manner of spiritual paraphernalia from elaborate alabaster altarpieces and sculptures of angels to rosary beads and postcard collections of Spanish saints and virgins.

Cafés

CAFÉ DE ORIENTE

Plaza de Oriente 2 Ⓜ Ópera. Mon–Thurs & Sun 8.30am–1.30am, Fri & Sat till 2.30am. MAP P.40, POCKET MAP A11

Elegant but pricey Parisian-style café with a popular terraza looking across the plaza to the palace. The café was opened in the 1980s by a priest, Padre Lezama, who ploughs his profits into various charitable schemes. There's an equally smart bar, *La Botilleria* (open noon–1am, an hour later on Fri & Sat), next door.

CHOCOLATERÍA SAN GINÉS

Pasadizo de San Ginés 11 Ⓜ Sol or Ópera Ⓦ chocolateriasangines.com. Daily 24hrs. MAP P.40, POCKET MAP C12

A Madrid institution, this café, established in 1894, serves *chocolate con churros* (thick hot chocolate with deep-fried hoops of batter) to perfection – just the thing to finish off a night of excess. It's an almost compulsory Madrileño custom to end up here after the clubs close, before heading home for a shower and then off to work.

Restaurants

LA BOLA

C/Bola 5 Ⓜ Santo Domingo or Ópera ☏ 915 476 930, Ⓦ labola.es. Mon–Sat 1–4pm & 8.30–11pm, Sun 1–4pm. MAP P.40, POCKET MAP A10

Opened back in 1870, *La Bola* is renowned for its *cocido madrileño* (soup followed by chickpeas and a selection of meats; €20), cooked in the traditional way over a wood fire. Don't plan on doing anything energetic afterwards. They don't accept cards, and service can be a little brusque.

LA BOLA

EL BUEY

Plaza de la Marina Española 1 Ⓜ Santo Domingo or Ópera ☏ 915 413 041, Ⓦ restauranteelbuey.com. Mon–Sat 1–4pm & 9pm–midnight, Sun 1–4pm. MAP P.40, POCKET MAP C4

A meat-eaters' paradise, specializing in superb steak that you fry yourself on a hotplate. Great side dishes and home-made desserts, with a highly drinkable house red, all for around €35 per head.

CASA GALLEGA

C/Bordadores 11 Ⓜ Ópera or Sol ☏ 915 419 055, Ⓦ lacasagallega.com; also Plaza San Miguel 8 Ⓜ Ópera or Sol ☏ 915 473 055. Both daily noon–midnight. MAP P.40, POCKET MAP B12, C11

Two airy and welcoming *marisquerías* that have been importing seafood on overnight trains from Galicia since opening in 1915. Costs vary according to the market price of the fish or shellfish that you order. *Pulpo* (octopus) and *pimientos de Padrón* (small peppers, spiced up by the odd fiery one) are brilliantly done and relatively inexpensive. There are set menus for €40–60 a head.

ENTRE SUSPIRO Y SUSPIRO

C/Caños de Peral 3 Ⓜ Ópera ☎ 915 420 644, ⓦ entresuspiroysuspiro.com. Mon–Fri 2–5pm & 9–1am, Sat 9–1am. MAP P.40, POCKET MAP B10

Given Madrid's links with Latin America, this is one of surprisingly few decent Mexican restaurants in the city. Quesadillas, tacos and some imaginative takes on traditional dishes served up in pleasant surroundings, although it is rather cramped and prices are high at around €40 for a meal.

EL ESCARPÍN

C/Hileras 17 Ⓜ Ópera ☎ 915 599 957, ⓦ sidreriaelescarpin.com. Daily 9am–4.30pm & 8pm–midnight. MAP P.40, POCKET MAP C11

Reasonably-priced Asturian bar-restaurant offering regional specialities including *chorizo a la sidra* (chorizo with cider), *fabes con almejas* (beans with clams) and, of course, cider. Eat tapas at the bar or try the brick-lined dining room.

Bar

EL ANCIANO REY DE LOS VINOS

C/Bailén 19 Ⓜ Ópera ⓦ elancianoreydelos vinos.es. Mon & Wed–Sun 9.30am–11.30pm. MAP P.40, POCKET MAP C6

Traditional standing-room-only bar founded back in 1909, serving well-poured beer, *vermút*, a decent selection of wine and some good tapas.

Club

JOY MADRID

C/Arenal 11 Ⓜ Sol or Ópera ⓦ www.joy -eslava.com. Daily midnight–6am. €10–15 including first drink. MAP P.40, POCKET MAP C11

This long-standing club is one of the staples of the Madrid night scene. It has a busy schedule of sessions every day of the week, catering for everything from house to seventies disco. If you arrive early, there are discounts on the entry fee.

Live music

CAFÉ DE CHINITAS

C/Torija 7 Ⓜ Santo Domingo ☎ 915 595 135, ⓦ chinitas.com. Mon–Sat 7pm–midnight; shows at 8.15pm & 10.30pm. Drinks and show €36. MAP P.40, POCKET MAP C4

One of the oldest flamenco clubs in Madrid, hosting a dinner-dance spectacular. The music is authentic but keep an eye on how much you order as the bill can mount up very quickly indeed. Be sure to make an advance reservation.

LA COQUETTE

C/Hileras 14 Ⓜ Ópera. Daily 8pm–3am. Closed Aug. MAP P.40, POCKET MAP C11

A small, crowded basement jazz and blues bar, where people sit around watching the band perform on a tiny stage. Live acts Tuesday–Thursday and a jam session on Sunday.

CAFÉ DE CHINITAS

Rastro, Lavapiés and Embajadores

Lavapiés and Embajadores were originally tough, working-class districts built to accommodate the huge population growth of Madrid in the eighteenth and nineteenth centuries. Traditional sights are thin on the ground, but some original tenement blocks survive and the area is now famous for the Rastro street market. These *barrios* are also home to the *castizos* – authentic *Madrileños* – who can be seen decked out in traditional costume during local festivals. The character of these areas has changed, however, in recent years. Young Spaniards and large numbers of immigrants have arrived, meaning that Lavapiés and Embajadores are now Madrid's most racially mixed *barrios*, with teahouses, kebab joints and textile shops sitting alongside some of the most original bars and restaurants in the city. Petty crime can be a problem round here but the reality is not as dramatic as newspapers suggest.

IGLESIA COLEGIATA DE SAN ISIDRO

C/Toledo 37 ⓜ Tirso de Molina or La Latina. Daily 7.30am–1pm & 6–9pm. Tours Sat 11.30am. MAP PP.48–49, POCKET MAP C14

Built from 1622 to 1633, this enormous twin-towered church was originally the centre of the Jesuit Order in Spain. After Carlos III fell out with the Order in 1767, he redesigned the interior and dedicated it to the city's patron, San Isidro. Isidro's remains – and those of his equally saintly wife – were brought here in 1769 from the nearby **Iglesia de San Andrés** (see p.33). The church was the city's cathedral from 1886 until 1993 when the **Catedral de la Almudena** (see p.39) was completed. It has a single nave with ornate lateral chapels and an impressive altarpiece.

MERCADO DEL RASTRO

ⓜ La Latina. MAP PP.48–49, POCKET MAP D8

Every Sunday morning, the heaving mass of El Rastro fleamarket takes over Calle Ribera de Curtidores. On offer

SAN CAYETANO

is just about anything you might – or more likely might not – need, from old clothes and military surplus to caged birds and fine antiques. Real bargains are rare, but the atmosphere is enjoyable and the nearby bars are as good as any in the city. Petty theft is common, so keep a close eye on your belongings. If you're looking for something more upmarket, try the antiques shops in **Galerías Piquer** at C/Ribera de Curtidores 29, which are also open Sunday mornings.

ESTADIO VICENTE CALDERÓN

Paseo Virgen del Puerto 67 ⓜ Pirámides ☎ 902 260 403, ⓦ clubatleticodemadrid.com. Match tickets from €30; ☎ 902 530 500 and via the website. MAP PP.48–49, POCKET MAP B7

Home to **Atlético Madrid**, one of the city's two big-name football teams, this 54,000-capacity stadium is quite a sight, with its smoked-glass sides rising high above the Manzanares river. Atlético may not have tasted the glory experienced by rivals Real Madrid, but they still rank as one of Spain's biggest teams. The stadium houses a club shop (Mon–Fri 10am–2pm & 2–8pm, Sat & Sun 10am–2pm, match days 11am–45 mins before kickoff) and a museum

(Tues–Sun 11am–7pm; €6; €3 under-12s. Guided tours Tues–Fri 1pm & 5.30pm, Sat & Sun noon, 1pm, 4.30pm & 5.30pm, depending on match times; €10; €15 under-12s) detailing the club's history and successes.

LA CORRALA

C/Tribulete 12 ⓜ Lavapiés. MAP PP.48–49, POCKET MAP E8

Built in 1839 and restored in the 1980s, this is one of many traditional *corrales* (tenement blocks) in Lavapiés, with balconied apartments opening onto a central patio. Plays, especially farces and *zarzuelas* (a mix of classical opera and music-hall), used to be performed regularly in *corrales*; this one usually hosts summer performances.

SAN CAYETANO

C/Embajadores 15 ⓜ Tirso de Molina or La Latina. Variable hours, usually Mon–Sat 9.30am–noon & 6–8pm, Sun 9am–2pm & 6–8pm. MAP PP.48–49, POCKET MAP E8

José de Churriguera and Pedro de Ribera, both renowned for their extravagant designs, were involved in the design of the elaborate facade, which dates from 1761. Most of the rest of the church was destroyed in the Civil War and has since been rebuilt.

PLAZA LAVAPIÉS

Ⓜ Lavapiés. MAP PP.48-49, POCKET MAP F8

In the Middle Ages, bustling Plaza Lavapiés was the core of Jewish Madrid, with the synagogue situated on the site now occupied by the Teatro Valle-Inclán. Today, with its Chinese, Arabic and African inhabitants, it remains a cosmopolitan place, and the plaza, along with Calle Argumosa running off from its southeastern corner, is an animated spot, with a variety of bars and cafés.

CALLE ATOCHA

Ⓜ Atocha or Antón Martín. MAP PP.48-49, POCKET MAP E6-H8

Calle Atocha, one of the old ceremonial routes from Plaza Mayor to the basilica at Atocha, forms the northeastern border of Lavapiés. At its southern end

it's a mishmash of fast-food and touristy restaurants, developing, as you move north up the hill, into a strange mixture of cheap hostels, fading shops, bars, lottery kiosks and sex emporia. With its brash neon lighting and shiny black facade, the huge sex shop at no. 80, El Mundo Fantástico, stands unashamedly opposite a convent and the site of an old printing house that produced the first edition of the first part of *Don Quixote*.

CINE DORÉ

C/Santa Isabel 3 Ⓜ Antón Martín ☎ 914 672 600. Closed Mon. Films €2.50. MAP PP.48-49, POCKET MAP F14

At the end of the narrow Pasaje Doré alley is the Cine Doré, the **oldest cinema** in Madrid. Dating from 1922 with a later Modernista/Art Nouveau

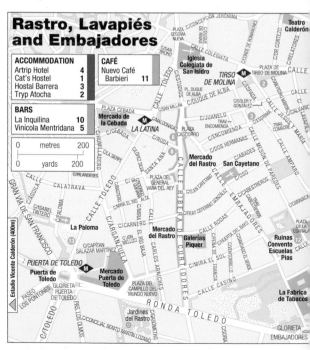

Rastro, Lavapiés and Embajadores

ACCOMMODATION	
Artrip Hotel	4
Cat's Hostel	1
Hostal Barrera	3
Tryp Atocha	2

CAFÉ	
Nuevo Café Barbieri	11

BARS	
La Inquilina	10
Vinícola Mentridana	5

facade, it's now the **Filmoteca Nacional**, an art-house cinema with bargain prices and a pleasant, inexpensive café/restaurant (Tues–Sun 4–11pm).

MUSEO DEL FERROCARRIL

Paseo de las Delicias 61 🚇 Delicias ☎ 902 228 822, 🌐 museodelferrocarril.org. Tues–Fri 9.30am–3pm, Sat & Sun 10am–3pm; closed Aug 16–31; €6, 4-12 yr olds €4; €2.50 on Sun. MAP PP.48-49, POCKET MAP H9

The Museo del Ferrocarril (Railway Museum) contains an impressive assortment of engines, carriages and wagons that once graced the train lines of Spain. The museum, which is housed in the handsome old station of Delicias, also has a fascinating collection of **model railways** and there's an atmospheric little café in one of the more elegant carriages.

CINE DORÉ

CLUB	
El Juglar	2

LIVE MUSIC	
Casa Patas	1

RESTAURANTS	
Asador Arizmendi	2
Los Chuchis	14
Gau Café	12
Malacatín	8
La Sanabresa	1
Taberna El Sur	4

TAPAS BARS	
Casa Amadeo "Los Caracoles"	6
Cervecería "Los Caracoles"	13
Freiduría de Gallinejas	15
Melo's	9
La Musa Espronceda	7
Taberna de Antonio Sánchez	3

Café

NUEVO CAFÉ BARBIERI

C/Ave María 45 Ⓜ Lavapiés. Tues & Wed 4pm–midnight, Thurs 4pm–1.30am, Fri & Sat 4pm–2.30am, Sun 4–11.30pm. MAP PP.48–49, POCKET MAP F8

A relaxed, slightly dilapidated café, with unobtrusive music, wooden tables, newspapers and a wide selection of coffees.

Restaurants

ASADOR ARIZMENDI

Plaza Tirso de Molina 7, 1° (entrance on C/Jesus y Maria) Ⓜ Tirso de Molina ☎ 914 295 030, Ⓦ asadorarizmendi.com. Tues–Sat 1–4pm & 9pm–midnight, Sun 1–4pm. Closed Aug. MAP PP.48–49, POCKET MAP D14

This charming neighbourhood restaurant is the locals' choice for long lunches. There's a range of delicious Castilian dishes and fine home-made desserts. There's a €25 lunchtime special menu; you'll pay €40–45 during the evening.

LOS CHUCHIS

C/Amparo 82 Ⓜ Lavapiés ☎ 911 276 606, Ⓦ facebook.com/LosChuchisBar. Tues–Thurs 11am–midnight, Fri 11am–12.30am, Sat noon–12.30am, Sun noon–8pm. MAP PP.48–49, POCKET MAP F8

Run by Brit Scott Preston, this gastro bar is a welcoming place serving some really great food. The menú del día is a great value €11.50 and features options such as hake with pesto and a selection of very tasty soups.

GAU CAFÉ

Edificio Escuelas Pias, C/Tribulete 14, 4° Ⓜ Lavapiés ☎ 915 282 594, Ⓦ gaucafe.com. Mon–Fri 11am–midnight, Sat & hols 1.30pm–midnight, closed Sun. MAP PP.48–49, POCKET MAP E8

Fabulous creative tapas-style dishes such as fried aubergines in rosemary honey and some really tasty chocolate desserts at this rooftop restaurant. It is not easy to find, though; make your way up past the library to the top floor. Menus €12.80 (lunch); €28 (evening). Cash only.

MALACATÍN

C/Ruda 5 Ⓜ La Latina ☎ 913 655 241, Ⓦ malacatin.com. Mon–Sat 11am–5.30pm, Thurs & Fri also open 8.15–11pm. Closed July 13–Aug 21. MAP PP.48–49, POCKET MAP D8

Established in 1895 to serve wine to local workmen, this authentic castizo restaurant serves generous helpings of arguably the best cocido in the city for a reasonable €19.50. Sample it at the bar for €5 too.

LA SANABRESA

C/Amor de Diós 12 Ⓜ Antón Martín ☎ 914 290 338. Mon–Sat 1–4.30pm & 8.30–11.30pm, Fri & Sat till midnight. Closed Aug. MAP PP.48–49, POCKET MAP G14

Unpretentious local comedor with reasonably priced dishes. There is a menú del día for around €11. Don't miss the grilled aubergines.

TABERNA EL SUR

C/Torrecilla del Leal 12 Ⓜ Antón Martín. Tues–Thurs 8pm–midnight, Fri & Sat noon–2am, Sun 1.30–5pm. MAP PP.48–49, POCKET MAP F7

Friendly bar/restaurant with an interesting array of good-value raciones including ropa vieja (Cuban-style beef) and curried chicken. A good wine selection and a welcoming atmosphere.

Tapas bars

CASA AMADEO "LOS CARACOLES"

Plaza Cascorro 18 Ⓜ La Latina. Tues–Fri 11am–4pm, Sat 11am–4pm & 7–10pm, Sun 10.30am–4pm. MAP PP.48–49, POCKET MAP D7

A favourite since the 1940s, with tapas from the eponymous caracoles (snails) to callos and oreja. It's heaving on Sundays, and keep an eye on the bill.

CERVECERÍA "LOS CARACOLES"

C/Toledo 106 Ⓜ Puerta de Toledo. Tues–Sat 9am–10.30pm, Sun 9am–4pm. Closed July.
MAP PP.48–49, POCKET MAP C8

Rough-and-ready bar specializing in snails, washed down with local *vermút del grifo* (draught vermouth).

FREIDURIA DE GALLINEJAS

C/Embajadores 84 Ⓜ Embajadores Ⓦ www .gallinejasembajadores.com. Daily 11am–11pm. Closed Aug. MAP PP.48–49, POCKET MAP F9

This traditional tiled, family-run bar is famed for serving the best fried lambs' intestines in the city. A variety of different cuts are available as well as straightforward fried lamb.

MELO'S

C/Ave María 44 Ⓜ Lavapiés. Tues–Sat 8pm–1am. Closed Aug. MAP PP.48–49, POCKET MAP F8

Standing room only at this very popular Galician bar serving huge *zapatillas* (bread filled with *lacón* – shoulder of pork – and cheese) plus great *pimientos de Padrón*.

LA MUSA ESPRONCEDA

C/Santa Isabel 17 Ⓜ Atocha or Antón Martín. Daily 1.30–4pm & 8pm–midnight. MAP PP.48–49, POCKET MAP G7

Great value tapas – classics such as tortilla and *croquetas* and creative bites such as brie wrapped in bacon – served in this friendly Lavapiés local. Offers a €10 lunchtime menu.

TABERNA DE ANTONIO SÁNCHEZ

C/Mesón de Paredes 13 Ⓜ Tirso de Molina Ⓦ tabernaantoniosanchez.com. Mon–Sat noon–4pm & 8pm–midnight, Sun noon–4.30pm. MAP PP.48–49, POCKET MAP E7

Said to be Madrid's oldest *taberna*, this seventeenth-century bar has a stuffed bull's head (in honour of the founder's son, who was killed by one) and a wooden interior. Lots of *finos*, plus *jamón* tapas or *tortilla de San Isidro* (salt cod omelette).

Bars

LA INQUILINA

C/Ave María 39 Ⓜ Lavapiés Ⓦ lainquilina.es. Tues–Thurs 7pm–2am, Fri–Sun 1–4pm & 8pm–3am. MAP PP.48–49, POCKET MAP F8

Once an old furniture shop, now a mainstay on the Lavapiés bar scene, *La Inquilina* is a deceptively large, bohemian bar that hosts regular art exhibitions and acoustic concerts. It serves a very decent range of tapas, too.

VINÍCOLA MENTRIDANA

C/San Eugenio 9 Ⓜ Antón Martín. Mon–Thurs & Sun 1pm–1am, Fri & Sat 1pm–2am. Closed Aug. MAP PP.48–49, POCKET MAP G7

Atmospheric traditional wine bar lined with dusty old bottles, a favourite with the Lavapiés crowd. An excellent selection of wine and well poured beer, plus appetising canapés and tapas.

Club

EL JUGLAR

C/Lavapiés 37 Ⓜ Lavapiés Ⓦ salajuglar.com. Wed–Sun 9.30pm–3am, Fri & Sat till 3.30am. MAP PP.48–49, POCKET MAP F8

Down-to-earth club with DJs playing funk and soul. There are also regular concerts with an entry fee of €6–13.

Live music

CASA PATAS

C/Cañizares 10 Ⓜ Antón Martín or Tirso Molina ☎ 913 690 496 Ⓦ casapatas.com. Shows: Mon–Thurs 10.30pm, Fri & Sat 9pm & midnight. €35. MAP PP.48–49, POCKET MAP E14

Authentic flamenco club with a bar and restaurant that gets its share of big names. The best nights are Thursday and Friday – check website for schedules.

Sol, Santa Ana and Huertas

The busy streets around Puerta del Sol, Plaza Santa Ana and Huertas are the bustling heart of Madrid and the reference point for most visitors to the capital. The city began to expand here during the sixteenth century and the area subsequently became known as the *barrio de las letras* (literary neighbourhood) because of the many authors and playwrights – including Cervantes – who made it their home. Today, the literary theme continues, with theatres, bookshops and cafés proliferating alongside the Círculo de Bellas Artes (Fine Arts Institute), the Teatro Español (historic theatre specializing in classic works) and the Congreso de Los Diputados (Parliament). For art lovers, there's the Real Academia de Bellas Artes de San Fernando museum, but for most visitors the main attraction is the vast array of traditional bars, particularly concentrated around the picturesque Plaza Santa Ana.

PUERTA DEL SOL

Sol. MAP P.54, POCKET MAP D11

This half-moon-shaped plaza, thronged with people at almost any hour of the day, marks the epicentre of Madrid and, indeed, of Spain – **Kilometre Zero**, an inconspicuous stone slab on the south side of the square, is the spot from which all distances in the country are measured. Opposite is an equestrian bronze of King Carlos III, and to the east a statue of Madrid's emblem, *el oso y el madroño* (bear and strawberry tree).

The square has been a popular meeting place since the mid-sixteenth century, when it was the site of one of the main

PUERTA DEL SOL

gates into the city. Its most important building is the Casa de Correos, built in 1766 and originally the city's post office. Under Franco it became the headquarters of the much-feared security police and it now houses the main offices of the Madrid regional government. The Neoclassical facade is crowned by the nation's most famous clock which officially ushers in the New Year: on December 31, *Madrileños* pack Puerta del Sol and attempt to scoff twelve grapes – one on each of the chimes of midnight – to bring themselves good luck for the next twelve months.

The square has also witnessed several incidents of national importance, including the slaughter of a rioting crowd by Napoleon's marshal, Murat, aided by the infamous Egyptian cavalry, on May 2, 1808. The massacre is depicted in Goya's canvas, *Dos de Mayo*, now hanging in the Prado (see p.66).

PLAZA SANTA ANA

PLAZA SANTA ANA

Ⓜ Sol or Antón Martín. MAP P.54, POCKET MAP F13

The main reason for visiting vibrant Plaza Santa Ana is the mass of bars, restaurants and cafés on the square itself and in the nearby streets that bring the area alive in the evenings.

The square was one of a series created by Joseph Bonaparte, whose passion for open spaces led to a remarkable remodelling of Madrid in the six short years of his reign. It's dominated by two distinguished buildings at either end: to the west, the *ME Madrid Reina Victoria*, a giant white confection of a hotel; to the east, the nineteenth-century Neoclassical Teatro Español. There has been a playhouse on this site since 1583, and the current theatre is the oldest in Madrid, its facade decorated with busts of famous Spanish playwrights.

CASA MUSEO LOPE DE VEGA

C/Cervantes 11 Ⓜ Antón Martín ⓦ casamuseolopedevega.org. Tues–Sun 10am–6pm. Free guided tours; wait for a group to be formed; ring ☎ 914 299 216 to reserve a tour in English. MAP P.54, POCKET MAP G13

Situated in the heart of the Huertas district, the reconstructed home of the great Golden Age Spanish dramatist offers a fascinating glimpse of life in seventeenth-century Madrid. Lope de Vega, a prolific writer with a tangled private life, lived here for 25 years until his death in 1635 at the age of 72. The house itself has been furnished in authentic fashion using the inventory left at the writer's death and highlights include a chapel containing some of his relics, his study with a selection of contemporary books, an Arabic-style drawing room and a delightful courtyard garden.

Cervantes lived and died at no. 2 on the same street and though the original building has long gone, a plaque above a shop marks the site.

Sol, Santa Ana and Huertas

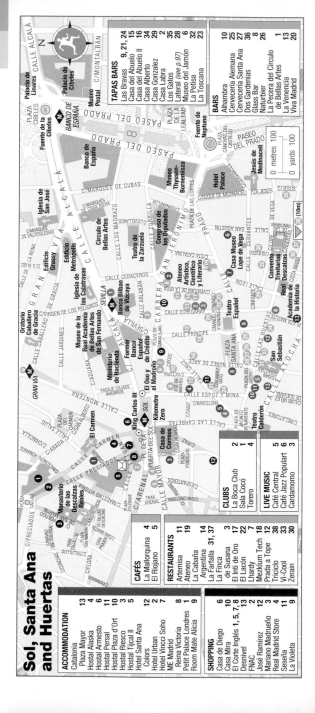

ACCOMMODATION

Catalonia	13
Plaza Mayor	4
Hostal Alaska	6
Hostal Armesto	11
Hostal Persal	10
Hostal Plaza d'Ort	3
Hostal Riesco	5
Hostal Tijcal II	
Hotel Santa Ana	12
Colors	7
Hotel Urban	
Hotel Vinci Soho	8
ME Madrid	1
Reina Victoria	9
Petit Palace Londres	
Room Mate Alicia	

SHOPPING

Casa de Diego	6
Casa Mira	10
El Corte Inglés	1, 5, 7, 8
Desnivel	13
FNAC	2
José Ramírez	12
Mariano Madrueño	4
Real Madrid Store	11
Seseña	9
La Violeta	

CAFÉS

La Mallorquina	4
El Riojano	5

RESTAURANTS

Artemisa	11
Ateneo	19
La Cabaña	
Argentina	14
La Farfalla	31, 37
La Finca	
de Susana	3
El Inti de Oro	17
El Lacón	22
Lhardy	7
Mezklum Tech	18
Prada a Tope	12
Triciclo	38
Vi-Cool	33
Zerain	30

CLUBS

La Boca Club	2
Sala Cocó	1
Torero	4

LIVE MUSIC

Café Central	5
Café Jazz Populart	6
Cardamomo	3

TAPAS BARS

Las Bravas	**9, 21, 24**
Casa del Abuelo	15
Casa del Abuelo II	16
Casa Alberto	34
Casa González	29
Casa Labra	2
Los Gatos	35
Lateral (see p.97)	28
Museo del Jamón	6
La Petisa	32
La Toscana	23

BARS

Alhambra	10
Cervecería Alemana	25
Cervecería Santa Ana	27
Dos Gardenias	36
Glass Bar	8
Naturbier	26
La Pecera del Círculo de Bellas Artes	1
La Venencia	13
Viva Madrid	20

0 metres 100

0 yards 100

ATENEO ARTÍSTICO, CIENTÍFICO Y LITERARIO

C/Prado 2 Ⓜ Antón Martín or Sevilla
Ⓦ ateneodemadrid.com. Tours Mon–Fri
10am–1pm; €3; book via website. MAP P.54,
POCKET MAP G12

The Ateneo (literary, scientific and political club) was founded after the 1820 Revolution and provided a focus for the new liberal political ideas circulating at that time. The exterior is neo-Plateresque in style, while the inside features a Neoclassical lecture theatre, a wooden panelled corridor with portraits of past presidents of the club and a splendid reading room. It also has a café and hosts occasional exhibitions.

CONGRESO DE LOS DIPUTADOS

Plaza de las Cortes Ⓜ Sevilla Ⓦ www.congreso
.es. Sat 10.30am–12.30pm (bring passport).
Closed Aug & hols. MAP P.54, POCKET MAP G12

The lower house of the **Spanish parliament** meets in a rather unprepossessing nineteenth-century building; its most distinguished feature is the two bronze lions that guard the entrance, made from a melted-down cannon captured during the African War of 1859–60. Sessions can be visited by appointment only, though you can turn up and queue for a free tour on Saturday mornings. This takes in several important rooms and the chamber with the bullet holes left by mad Colonel Tejero and his Guardia Civil associates in the abortive coup of 1981.

CALLE ALCALÁ

Ⓜ Sol or Sevilla. MAP P.54, POCKET MAP E11–J10

An imposing catalogue of Spanish architecture lines Calle Alcalá, an ancient thoroughfare that originally led to the university town of Alcalá de Henares. It starts at Puerta del Sol; in this first stretch, look out particularly for the splendid early twentieth-century wedge-shaped Banco Español de Crédito adorned with **elephant heads** and plaques listing all the branches of the bank in Spain, soon to be turned into a luxury hotel, shopping centre and apartment block. The Banco de Bilbao Vizcaya, with its Neoclassical facade complete with charioteers on top, and thebaroque Ministerio de Hacienda (Inland Revenue) are similarly impressive.

IGLESIA DE SAN JOSÉ

C/Alcalá 41 Ⓜ Banco de España. Daily 7am–12.30pm & 6–8.30pm, Sun open from 9am. MAP P.54, POCKET MAP G10

The red-brick Iglesia de San José, near the junction with Gran Vía, dates back to the 1730s and was the last building designed by the prolific Pedro de Ribera. The interior holds the ornate Santa Teresa de Ávila chapel and an impressive collection of colourful images of Christ and the Virgin Mary.

IGLESIA DE LAS CALATRAVAS

C/Alcalá 25 Ⓜ Sevilla Ⓦ iglesiacalatravas .com. Mon–Fri 8am–1pm & 6–8pm, Sat 6.30–8pm, Sun 11am–1.30pm & 6.30–8pm. MAP P.54, POCKET MAP F11

The pastel-pink Iglesia de las Calatravas was built in the seventeenth century for the nuns of the Calatrava, one of the four Spanish military orders. Inside, it contains a fantastically elaborate gold altarpiece by José Churriguera.

MUSEO DE LA REAL ACADEMIA DE BELLAS ARTES DE SAN FERNANDO

C/Alcalá 13 Ⓜ Sevilla ☎ 915 240 864 Ⓦ realacademiabellasartessanfernando.com. Tues–Sun 10am–3pm. €6, free Wed. Closed Aug. MAP P.54, POCKET MAP F11

Established by Felipe V in 1744 and housed in its present location since 1773, the Museo de la Real Academia de Bellas Artes de San Fernando is one of the most important art galleries in Spain. Its displays include sections on sculpture, architecture and music, some interesting French and Italian work and an extraordinary – but chaotically displayed – collection of Spanish paintings, including El Greco, Velázquez, Murillo and Picasso.

The Goya section has two revealing self-portraits, several depictions of the despised royal favourite *Don Manuel Godoy*, the desolate representation of *The Madhouse* and *The Burial of the Sardine* (a popular procession that continues to this day in Madrid).

The gallery also holds the national copper engraving collection (Mon–Thurs 9am–5pm, Fri 9am–3pm; free), which includes Goya etchings and several of the copper plates used for his *Capricho* series on show in the Prado.

CÍRCULO DE BELLAS ARTES

C/Marqués de Casa Riera 2 Ⓜ Banco de España Ⓦ circulobellasartes.com. Exhibitions Tues–Sat 11am–2pm & 5–9pm, Sun 11am–2pm. €3. MAP P.54, POCKET MAP G11

REAL ACADEMIA DE BELLAS ARTES DE SAN FERNANDO

This striking 1920s Art Deco building, crowned by a statue of Pallas Athene, is home to one of Madrid's best arts centres. Inside, there's a theatre, music hall, galleries, cinema and café bar (see p.64). For many years a stronghold of Spain's intelligentsia, it attracts the city's arts and media crowd but is not exclusive, nor expensive. As the Círculo is theoretically a members-only club, it issues day membership on the door.

PLAZA DE CIBELES

Ⓜ Banco de España. MAP P.54, POCKET MAP J10

Encircled by four of the most monumental buildings in Madrid, Plaza de Cibeles is one of the city's most famous landmarks. At its centre, and marooned in a sea of never-ending traffic, is the late eighteenth-century fountain and statue of the goddess Cybele riding in a lion-drawn chariot. Built to celebrate the city's first public water supply, today the fountain is the post-victory congregation point for Real Madrid fans (Atlético supporters bathe in the fountain of Neptune just down the road).

PALACIO DE CIBELES

Ⓜ Banco de España Ⓦ centrocentro.org. Exhibitions Tues–Sun 10am–8pm. MAP P.54, POCKET MAP J10

This grandiose wedding-cake of a building on the eastern side of Paseo del Prado, constructed between 1904 and 1917 by the prolific architect partnership of Antonio Palacios and Joaquín Otamendi, was once Madrid's main post office, but has recently been usurped by the Madrid City Council. It is now home to a smart exhibition space, a viewing gallery (Tues–Sun 10am–8pm; €2,

under-12s €0.50), a café (daily 10am-midnight), expensive restaurant run by Toledan restaurateur Adolfo Muñoz, and an overpriced and rather *pijo* terrace bar (daily 10am–2am), which does offer some great views over the Paseo del Prado.

PALACIO DE LINARES

Plaza de Cibeles 2 Ⓜ Banco de España Ⓦ www.casamerica.es. Exhibitions usually Mon-Sat 11am-8pm, Sun 11am-3pm; guided tours Sat & Sun 11am, noon, 1pm. €8, students and over-65s €5, under-12s free. Closed Aug. MAP P.54, POCKET MAP J10

This palatial eighteenth-century mansion, built by the Marqués de Linares, is now home to the Casa de América, a cultural organization that promotes Latin American art through concerts, films and exhibitions. At weekends, there are guided tours through the sumptuous mansion decorated with some marvellous frescoes, crystal chandeliers and elaborate tapestries from the Real Fábrica (see p.76). The palacio also has an expensive designer restaurant and an excellent summer garden terrace.

Shops

CASA DE DIEGO

Puerta del Sol 12 Ⓜ Sol Ⓦ casadediego
.com. Mon–Sat 9.30am–8pm. MAP P.54,
POCKET MAP E11

Old-time shop with helpful
staff selling a fabulous array
of Spanish fans (*abanicos*)
ranging from cheap offerings
at under €12 to beautifully
hand-crafted works of art
costing up to €1500. Sells
umbrellas, walking sticks and
shawls too.

CASA MIRA

Carrera de San Jerónimo 30 Ⓜ Sevilla
Ⓦ casamira.es. Daily 10am–2pm & 5–9pm.
Closed mid-July to Sept. MAP P.54,
POCKET MAP F12

The place to go for *turrón*
(flavoured nougat, eaten by
Spaniards at Christmas) and
marzipan. The family business
has been open for over a 150
years since the founder, Luis
Mira, arrived from Asturias
and set up a stall in Puerta
del Sol.

EL CORTE INGLÉS

C/Preciados 1–4 Ⓜ Sol & Plaza Callao 2
Ⓜ Callao. Mon–Sat 10am–9pm & first Sun in
the month. MAP P.54, POCKET MAP D10 & D11

The Spanish department store
par excellence. It's not cheap,
but the quality is very good, the
staff are highly professional
(the majority speak English)
and there's a gourmet section
on the ninth floor of the Callao
branch with fantastic views
over the city (see p.88).

DESNIVEL

Plaza Matute 6 Ⓜ Antón Martín Ⓦ libreria
desnivel.com. Mon–Fri 10am–8.30pm, Sat
11am–8.30pm. MAP P.54, POCKET MAP F14

A great selection of maps and
guides if you fancy a hike in
the nearby Sierra Guadarrama.

FNAC

C/Preciados 28 Ⓜ Callao Ⓦ fnac.es.
Mon–Sat 10am–9.30pm, Sun
11.30am–9.30pm. MAP P.54, POCKET MAP D10

Department store with sections
for books, videos, CDs and
electrical equipment. Also sells
concert tickets.

JOSÉ RAMÍREZ

C/Paz 8 Ⓜ Sol Ⓦ guitarrasramirez.com.
Mon–Fri 10am–2pm & 5–8pm, Sat
10am–2pm. MAP P.54, POCKET MAP D12

The Ramírez family have been
making handcrafted guitars
since 1882 and, even if you
are not a budding flamenco
artist, this beautiful old shop
is still worth a visit to
appreciate these works of art
used by some of the world's
leading musicians.

CASA DE DIEGO

MARIANO MADRUEÑO

C/Postigo San Martín 3 ⓂCallao
ⓦmarianomadrueno.es. Mon–Fri
9.30am–2pm & 5–8pm, Sat 9.30am–2pm.
MAP P.54, POCKET MAP C10

Traditional wine seller's, established in 1895, where there's an overpowering smell of grapes as you peruse its vintage-crammed shelves. Intriguing tipples include potent Licor de Hierbas from Galicia and home-made Pacharán (aniseed liqueur with sloe berries).

REAL MADRID STORE

C/Carmen 3 ⓂSol. Mon–Sat 10am–9pm,
Sun 11am–8pm. MAP P.54, POCKET MAP D11

Club store where you can pick up replica shirts and all manner of – expensive – souvenirs related to the club's history. There is another branch in the shopping centre on the corner of Real's Bernabéu stadium (see p.93) at C/Padre Damian Puerta 55.

SESEÑA

C/Cruz 23 ⓂSol ⓦsesena.com. Mon–Sat
10am–1.30pm & 4.30–8pm. MAP P.54,
POCKET MAP E12

Open since 1901, this shop specializes in traditional Madrileño capes for royalty and celebrities. Clients have included Luis Buñuel, Gary Cooper and Hillary Clinton.

LA VIOLETA

Plaza de Canalejas 6 ⓂSol/Sevilla.
Mon–Sat 10am–2pm & 4.30–8.30pm.
Closed Aug. MAP P.54, POCKET MAP F12

Old-style confectionary store founded in 1915 and famous for its *violetas*, delicate sweets made from the essence of the violet flower. They also sell violet marmalade, honey and tea as well as more traditional delights for the sweet-toothed.

SESEÑA

Cafés

LA MALLORQUINA

Puerta del Sol 2 ⓂSol ⓦpasteleria
mallorquina.es. Daily 9am–9.15pm. MAP P.54,
POCKET MAP D12

Classic Madrid café, great for breakfast or sweet snacks. Try one of their *napolitanas* (cream slices) in the upstairs salon that overlooks Puerta del Sol.

EL RIOJANO

C/Mayor 10 ⓂSol ⓦconfiteriaelriojano
.com. Daily 10am–2am & 5–9pm. MAP P.54,
POCKET MAP D12

Traditional patisserie shop and café selling a wonderful range of Spanish-style sweets and cakes, such as *buñuelos de viento* (balls of chocolate, custard or cream covered in batter) and *torrijas* (bread cooked in milk, egg, sugar, cinnamon and lemon).

Restaurants

ARTEMISA

C/Ventura de la Vega 4 ⓂSevilla ☎914 295
092, ⓦrestaurantesvegetarianosartemisa.com.
Daily 1.30–4pm & 9pm–midnight. MAP P.54,
POCKET MAP F12

Long-standing vegetarian restaurant, serving a wide range of dishes including courgettes with curry and raisins. There is a good value set lunch for €11.90.

ATENEO

C/Santa Catalina 10 Ⓜ Sol/Sevilla ☎ 914 202 432, Ⓦ restauranteateneo.es. Mon–Sat 9am–1am, Sun 9am–10pm. MAP P.54, POCKET MAP G12

Smartly decorated café/restaurant sharing its name with the literary club to which it is connected (see p.55). It specializes in well prepared traditional Spanish dishes with an international twist served up in pleasant surroundings. There is a very decent €15 set lunch on weekdays.

LA CABAÑA ARGENTINA

C/Ventura de la Vega 10 Ⓜ Sevilla ☎ 913 697 202, Ⓦ lacabanaargentina.es. Mon–Thurs & Sun 1.15pm–midnight, Fri & Sat 1.30pm–12.30am. MAP P.54, POCKET MAP F12

One of the best Argentine eateries in the city. Excellent-quality meat (*el bife lomo alto* is a house favourite) and classic desserts including *panqueques*. Friendly service and only around €35 a head.

LA FARFALLA

C/Santa María 17 Ⓜ Antón Martín ☎ 913 694 391, Ⓦ lafarfalla.es. Tues–Fri 8.30pm–late, Sat & Sun 1–4pm & 8.30pm–late. MAP P.54, POCKET MAP G14

Deservedly popular Italian-Argentine restaurant, one of the stalwarts of the Huertas scene.

MEZKLUM TECH

There's a fantastic selection of pizzas (€7–8) and Argentine meats (the €18.75 *parrillada* serves two), and very appetising home-made desserts. As well as being good value, it is also open especially late: a good option if you suffer from late-night hunger pangs. Another branch nearby at C/Huertas 6.

LA FINCA DE SUSANA

C/Arlabán 4 Ⓜ Sevilla. Daily 1–3.45pm & 8.30–11.45pm. MAP P.54, POCKET MAP F11

One of three good-value restaurants set up by a group of Catalan friends (another, *La Gloria de Montera*, is just off Gran Vía). A varied *menú del día* for around €10 consists of simple dishes cooked with a little imagination. Efficient but impersonal service. You can't book, so arrive early to avoid queueing.

EL INTI DE ORO

C/Ventura de la Vega 12 Ⓜ Antón Martín ☎ 914 296 703, Ⓦ intideoro.com. Daily 1.30–4pm & 8.30pm–midnight. Also at C/Amor de Dios 9 Ⓜ Antón Martín ☎ 914 291 958. MAP P.54, POCKET MAP F12

The friendly staff at this good-value Peruvian restaurant are more than ready to provide suggestions for those new to the cuisine. The pisco sour, a cocktail of Peruvian liquor, lemon juice, egg white and sugar is a recommended starter, while the *ceviche de merluza* (raw fish marinated in lemon juice) is a wonderful dish. A full meal costs around €30.

EL LACÓN

C/Manuel Fernández y González 8 Ⓜ Sol ☎ 914 296 042, Ⓦ mesonellacon.com. Daily 1–4pm & 8pm–midnight. Closed Aug. MAP P.54, POCKET MAP F12

A large Galician bar-restaurant with plenty of seats upstairs. Great *pulpo*, *caldo gallego* (meat and vegetable broth) and *empanadas*. They also do a neat *menú exprés* at lunchtime consisting of a single course and a drink for just €4.

LHARDY

Carrera de San Jerónimo 8 Ⓜ Sol ☎ 915 213 385. Restaurant: Mon–Sat 1–3.30pm & 9–11.30pm, Sun 1–3.30pm. Shop: Mon–Sat 8am–3pm & 5–9.30pm, Sun 9am–2.30pm. Closed Aug. MAP P.54, POCKET MAP E12

Once the haunt of royalty, this is one of Madrid's most beautiful and famous restaurants. It's greatly overpriced – expect to pay over €60 per head for a three-course meal – but on the ground floor, there's a wonderful bar/shop where you can have breakfast or snack on canapés, *fino* and consommé, without breaking the bank.

MEZKLUM TECH

C/Príncipe 16 Ⓜ Sevilla ☎ 915 218 911. Mon–Thurs 1.30–4pm & 9pm–12.30am, Fri & Sat 1.30–4.30pm & 9pm–1am, Sun 1.30–4.30pm. MAP P.54, POCKET MAP F12

A self-consciously cool, chic arrival on the Santa Ana scene decked out in minimalist style with white, pink and lilac tones. Serves a fine array of Mediterranean dishes with good salads and pasta. It has a lunchtime menu at €10.70 and two evening menus at €20 and €25.

PRADA A TOPE

C/Príncipe 11 Ⓜ Sol ☎ 914 295 921. Tues–Sun 12.30–5pm & 8pm–midnight. MAP P.54, POCKET MAP F12

Quality produce from the El Bierzo region of León. The *morcilla* (black pudding), *empanada* (pasty) and tortilla are extremely tasty, while the smooth house wines provide the ideal accompaniment.

TRICICLO

C/Santa María 28 Ⓜ Antón Martín ☎ 910 244 798. Ⓦ triciclo.es. Mon–Sat 1.30–4pm & 8.30–midnight. MAP P.54, POCKET MAP G14

LHARDY

With its distinctive red-fronted facade, this popular restaurant in the heart of Huertas is garnering a reputation for quality *raciones* such as steak tartar, roast cod or oxtail ravioli, from around €15 per dish.

VI-COOL

C/Huertas 12 Ⓜ Antón Martín ☎ 914 294 913. Ⓦ vi-cool.com. Daily 1–4pm & 8pm–midnight. MAP P.54, POCKET MAP F13

Catalan celebrity chef Sergi Arola's latest and most affordable venture in Madrid. The low-key, minimalist interior is the setting for some simple but classy and creative offerings including spinach cannelloni, fried langoustines in a curry and mint sauce, and gourmet hamburgers and pizzas. There are tapas selections at €20 and €35.

ZERAIN

C/Quevedo 3 Ⓜ Antón Martín ☎ 914 297 909. Mon–Sat 1.30–4pm & 8.30pm–midnight. Closed Aug. MAP P.54, POCKET MAP G13

Basque cider house serving excellent meat and fish dishes. The *chuletón* (T-bone steak) is the speciality, but it also does a very good *tortilla de bacalao* and grilled *rape* (monkfish). Three courses are around €40.

Tapas bars

LAS BRAVAS

C/Alvarez Gato 3 Ⓜ Sol. Other branches at C/Espoz y Mina 13 Ⓜ Sol; & Pasaje Mathéu 5 Ⓜ Sol. Daily 12.30–4.30pm & 8.30pm–midnight. MAP P.54, POCKET MAP E12 & E13

Standing room only at these three bars, where, as the name suggests, *patatas bravas* are the thing – they patented their own version of the spicy sauce.

CASA ALBERTO

C/Huertas 18 Ⓜ Antón Martín ☎ 914 299 356, Ⓦ casaalberto.es. Daily noon–1.30am, Sun noon–4pm (in summer). Closed July & Aug. MAP P.54, POCKET MAP F13

Traditional *tasca* that has resisted the passage of time since it was founded back in 1827. Good *caracoles* (snails), *gambas* (prawns) and great *croquetas*, ideally accompanied by a glass of house vermouth.

CASA DEL ABUELO

C/Victoria 12 Ⓜ Sol Ⓦ lacasadelabuelo.es. Daily noon–midnight (Fri & Sat until 1am). MAP P.54, POCKET MAP E12

A tiny, atmospheric bar serving just their own cloyingly sweet red wine (stick with a beer instead) and delicious cooked prawns – try them *al ajillo* (in garlic) or *a la plancha* (fried) – which are fried up in the tiny corner kitchen.

CASA DEL ABUELO II

C/Núñez de Arce 5 Ⓜ Sol Ⓦ lacasadelabuelo .es. Daily noon–midnight (Fri & Sat until 1am). MAP P.54, POCKET MAP E12

There's a *comedor* (dining room) at the back of this classic Madrid bar, with a selection of traditional *raciones* – the *croquetas* are great – and a jug of house wine.

CASA GONZÁLEZ

C/León 12 Ⓜ Antón Martín. MAP P.54, POCKET MAP F13

Friendly delicatessen/tapas bar with an extensive range of wines and cheese and serving up some great tapas including a fantastic *salmorejo*, speciality sausage from around Spain and some imaginative *tostas* covered in a variety of patés.

CASA LABRA

C/Tetuán 12 Ⓜ Sol ☎ 915 310 081, Ⓦ casalabra.es. Daily 9.30am–3.30pm & 5.30–11pm. MAP P.54, POCKET MAP D11

Dating from 1869 – and where the Spanish Socialist Party was founded ten years later – this traditional and highly popular

CASA ALBERTO

place retains much of its original interior. Order a drink at the bar and a *ración* of *bacalao* (cod fried in batter) or some of the best *croquetas* in town. There's also a restaurant at the back serving classic Madrileño food. Be prepared to queue.

LOS GATOS

C/Jesús 2, Ⓜ Antón Martín. Mon–Thurs & Sun 11am–1am, Fri & Sat 11am–2am. MAP P.54, POCKET MAP H13

Decorated with a multifarious collection of curiosities including a model of a choirboy with sunglasses, a jazz musician and a horned gramophone, this old-style bar serves up an excellent selection of canapés and beer for its loyal clientele.

MUSEO DEL JAMÓN

Carrera de San Jerónimo 6 Ⓜ Sol Ⓦ museo deljamon.com. Mon–Sat 9am–midnight, Sun 10am–midnight. MAP P.54, POCKET MAP E12

This is the largest branch of this unpretentious Madrid chain, from whose ceilings are suspended hundreds of *jamones* (hams). The best – and they're not cheap – are the *jabugos* from the Sierra Morena, though a filling ham sandwich is only around €2.

LA PETISA

C/Lope de Vega 15 Ⓜ Antón Martín Ⓦ lapetisabar.com. Tues–Thurs 1pm–4.30pm & 7pm–midnight, Fri & Sat 1pm–1.30am, Sun 1–6pm. MAP P.54, POCKET MAP G13

Carving out a niche for itself in the highly competitive tapas market is this friendly little bar, which serves some delicious Argentine-influenced dishes such as *empanadillas*, plus gourmet hamburgers, very good salads and a delicious carrot cake for dessert.

LA TOSCANA

C/Manuel Fernández y González 10 Ⓜ Antón Martín or Sevilla. Tues–Sat 1–4pm & 8pm– midnight. Closed Aug. MAP P.54, POCKET MAP F12

This popular and friendly Huertas classic serves up some delicious home-made tapas. The *morcillo* (beef shank) is excellent, while the *croquetas*, *chistorra* and tuna salads are also very tasty.

Bars

ALHAMBRA

C/Victoria 9 Ⓜ Sol. Daily 11am–1.30am (2am at weekends). MAP P.54, POCKET MAP E12

Friendly tapas bar by day, fun disco bar by night, with the crowds spilling over into the *El Buscón* bar next door.

CERVECERÍA ALEMANA

Plaza de Santa Ana 6 Ⓜ Sol or Antón Martín
Ⓦ cerveceriaalemana.com. Mon & Wed–Sun
10.30am–12.30am, Fri & Sat 2am. Closed
Aug. MAP P.54, POCKET MAP F13

Traditional old beer house,
once frequented by Hemingway.
Order a *caña* (draught beer)
and go easy on the tapas, as the
bill can mount up fast.

CERVECERÍA SANTA ANA

Plaza de Santa Ana 10 Ⓜ Sol or Antón
Martín Ⓦ cerveceriasantaana.com. Daily
11am–1.30am, Fri & Sat till 2.30am. MAP P.54,
POCKET MAP F13

Has tables outside, and offers
quality beer, friendly service
and a good selection of tapas.
Always packed at night.

DOS GARDENIAS

C/Santa María 13 Ⓜ Antón Martín. Mon–Sat
9.30pm–2.30am, Sun 5pm–2.30am. MAP P.54,
POCKET MAP G14

Intimate and relaxed little bar in
the Huertas area where you can
chill out in their comfy chairs,
sip on a mojito, and escape from
the hubbub of the city outside.

GLASS BAR

Carrera San Jeronimo 34 Ⓜ Sevilla.
Mon–Wed & Sun 10.30–2am, Thurs–Sat
10.30–3am. MAP P.54, POCKET MAP F12

Housed in the ultra-chic *Hotel
Urban*, this glamorous cocktail
bar has become a favourite
with the well-heeled in-crowd.

Designer tapas such as sushi,
wild salmon and oysters
accompany drinks. In summer,
a terrace bar opens on the
sixth floor.

NATURBIER

Plaza de Santa Ana 9 Ⓜ Sol or Antón Martín
Ⓦ naturbier.com. Daily 8pm–2.30am. MAP P.54,
POCKET MAP F13

Try this place's own tasty beer
with a variety of German
sausages to accompany it. There's
usually room to sit in the cellar
if the top bar is too crowded,
although service is often slow.

LA PECERA DEL CÍRCULO DE BELLAS ARTES

C/Alcalá 42 Ⓜ Banco de España Ⓦ lapecera
delcirculo.com. Daily 8am–2am, Fri & Sat till
3am. MAP P.54, POCKET MAP G11

Stylish bar in this classy arts
centre (€1 entry fee), complete
with reclining nude sculpture,
chandeliers and sofas and a
pleasant lack of pretensions.
Service can be slow though.
From May to October, there's a
comfortable terraza outside.

LA VENENCIA

C/Echegaray 7 Ⓜ Sevilla. Daily 1–3.30pm
& 7.30pm–1.30am. Closed Aug. MAP P.54,
POCKET MAP F12

Rather dilapidated, wood-
panelled bar that's great for
sherry sampling. The whole
range is here, served from
wooden barrels, and

LA PECERA DEL CÍRCULO DE BELLAS ARTES

accompanied by delicious olives and *mojama* (dry salted tuna).

VIVA MADRID

C/Manuel Fernández y González 7 Ⓜ Antón Martín or Sevilla. Daily noon–2am, Fri & Sat till 3am. MAP P.54, POCKET MAP F12

A fabulous tiled bar with a popular terrace that is a longtime stalwart of the Madrid night scene. Refurbished and now offering a wide selection of food and tapas, but still best for a drink.

Clubs

LA BOCA CLUB

C/Echegaray 11 Ⓜ Antón Martín or Sevilla Ⓦ labocaclub.com. Wed–Sat 9.30pm–3am. MAP P.54, POCKET MAP F12

Dark, cavern-like club on this buzzing little street close to Santa Ana playing everything from electronic and funk to rock and salsa. Live gigs (in the dungeon-like cellar) and resident DJs.

SALA COCÓ

C/Alcalá 20 Ⓜ Sevilla. Thurs–Sat midnight–6am. MAP P.54, POCKET MAP F11

Über-modern decor in a slick club, one of the most fashionable stops of the night on the Madrid scene. Electronic sounds in the Mondo Disko sessions on Thursday and Saturday nights from midnight, popular house sessions on Fridays. Entry €20 (includes one drink).

TORERO

C/Cruz 26 Ⓜ Sol. Tues–Sat 10.30pm–5.30am (4.30am Wed). Entrance €10 including first drink. MAP P.54, POCKET MAP E13

Popular two-floored club right in the heart of the Santa Ana area. The bouncers are pretty strict, but once inside a fun place to be. Music ranges from salsa to disco.

GLASS BAR

Live music

CAFÉ CENTRAL

Plaza del Ángel 10 Ⓜ Tirso de Molina ☎ 913 694 143, Ⓦ cafecentralmadrid.com. Mon–Thurs 12.30pm–2.30am, Fri 12.30pm–3.30am, Sat 11.30am–3.30am, Sun 11.30pm–2.30am. €12–15 for gigs. MAP P.54, POCKET MAP E13

Small jazz club that gets the odd big name, plus strong local talent. The Art Deco café (lunchtime menu €12; €15 at weekends) is worth a visit in its own right.

CAFÉ JAZZ POPULART

C/Huertas 22 Ⓜ Tirso de Molina ☎ 914 298 407, Ⓦ populart.es. Daily 6pm–2.30am. Usually free. MAP P.54, POCKET MAP F13

Friendly and laidback venue, with twice-nightly sets (10pm & 11.15pm) usually from jazz and blues bands.

CARDAMOMO

C/Echegaray 15 Ⓜ Antón Martín or Sevilla ☎ 913 690 757, Ⓦ cardamomo.es. Mon & Wed–Sun 8pm–4am. Shows at 9pm. MAP P.54, POCKET MAP F12

This flamenco bar has evolved into a respected fully blown *tablao*. The show with a drink is €39, while dinner will set you back an extra €33. Check the website for the schedule.

Paseo del Arte and Retiro

Madrid's three world-class art galleries are all located within a kilometre of each other along what is known as the Paseo del Arte. The Prado, the most renowned of the three, houses an unequalled display of Spanish art, an outstanding Flemish collection and some impressive Italian work. The Thyssen-Bornemisza, based on one of the world's greatest private art collections, provides a dazzling excursion through Western art from the fourteenth to the late twentieth centuries. Finally, the Centro de Arte Reina Sofía displays contemporary art, including Picasso's iconic masterpiece *Guernica*. The area around the Paseo del Prado has two beautiful green spaces: the Jardines Botánicos and the Parque del Retiro, as well as lesser-known sights including the fascinating Real Fábrica de Tapices (Royal Tapestry Workshop) and the Museo Naval. It isn't an area renowned for its bars, restaurants and nightlife, but there are plenty of decent places for a drink or lunch.

MUSEO DEL PRADO

Ⓜ Atocha or Banco de España Ⓦ www
.museodelprado.es. Mon–Sat 10am–8pm,
Sun & hols 10am–7pm. €14, free Mon–Sat
6–8pm, Sun & hols 5–7pm and for under-18s.
MAP PP.66–69, POCKET MAP J13–14

The Prado is Madrid's premier tourist attraction and one of the oldest and greatest collections of art in the world, largely amassed by the Spanish royal family over the last two hundred years.

Tickets are purchased at the Puerta de Goya opposite the *Hotel Ritz* on C/Felipe IV and the entrance is round the back

GARDEN OF EARTHLY DELIGHTS

at the Puerta de los Jerónimos, which leads into the new extension. To avoid the large ticket queues, buy them from the museum website.

The museum, which was given a new lease of life following the addition of the controversial €152 million Rafael Moneo-designed extension, is set out according to national schools. To follow the route proposed by the museum, bear right upon entering and head into the central hallway, the Sala de las Musas; from here you are guided through the collections on the ground floor before being directed upstairs.

The coverage of Spanish paintings begins with some striking twelfth-century Romanesque frescoes. Beyond is a stunning anthology that includes just about every significant Spanish painter, from the adopted Cretan-born artist El Greco (Domenikos Theotokopoulos), who worked in Toledo in the 1570s, to Francisco de Goya, the outstanding painter of eighteenth-century Bourbon Spain. Don't miss the breathtaking collection of work by Diego Velázquez, including his masterpiece, Las Meninas.

No visit is complete without taking in Goya's deeply evocative works, Dos de Mayo and Tres de Mayo, and his disturbing series of murals known as the Pinturas Negras (Black Paintings) with their mix of witches, fights to the death and child-eating gods. The artist's remarkable versatility is clear when these are compared with his voluptuous portraits of the Maja Vestida (Clothed Belle) and Maja Desnuda (Naked Belle).

The Italian paintings include the most complete collection by painters from the Venice

MUSEO DEL PRADO

School in any single museum, among them Titian's magnificent equestrian portrait, Emperor Carlos V at Mühlberg. There are also major works by Raphael and epic masterpieces from Tintoretto, Veronese and Caravaggio.

The early Flemish works are even more impressive and contain one of Hieronymus Bosch's greatest triptychs, the hallucinogenic Garden of Earthly Delights. Look out, too, for the works of Pieter Bruegel the Elder, whose Triumph of Death must be one of the most frightening canvases ever painted, Rogier van der Weyden's magnificent Descent from the Cross and the extensive Rubens collection.

German and French painting is less well represented but still worth seeking out – especially the pieces by Dürer, Cranach and Poussin – while downstairs in the basement is a glittering display of the jewels that belonged to the Grand Dauphin Louis, son of Louis XIV and father of Felipe V, Spain's first Bourbon king.

The new wing houses temporary exhibition spaces, restoration workshops and a sculpture gallery as well as a restaurant, café and shops.

Paseo del Arte and Retiro

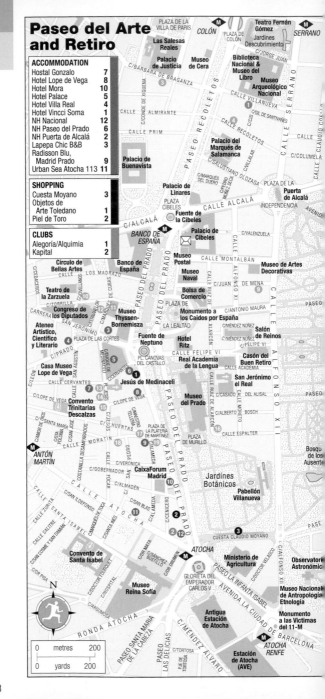

ACCOMMODATION

Hostal Gonzalo	7
Hotel Lope de Vega	8
Hotel Mora	10
Hotel Palace	5
Hotel Villa Real	4
Hotel Vincci Soma	1
NH Nacional	12
NH Paseo del Prado	6
NH Puerta de Alcalá	2
Lapepa Chic B&B	3
Radisson Blu, Madrid Prado	9
Urban Sea Atocha 113	11

SHOPPING

Cuesta Moyano	3
Objetos de Arte Toledano	1
Piel de Toro	2

CLUBS

Alegoría/Alquimia	1
Kapital	2

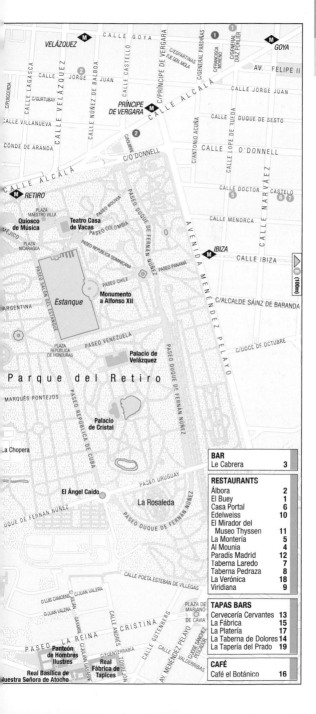

BAR	
Le Cabrera	3

RESTAURANTS	
Álbora	2
El Buey	1
Casa Portal	6
Edelweiss	10
El Mirador del Museo Thyssen	11
La Montería	5
Al Mounia	4
Paradís Madrid	12
Taberna Laredo	7
Taberna Pedraza	8
La Verónica	18
Viridiana	9

TAPAS BARS	
Cervecería Cervantes	13
La Fábrica	15
La Platería	17
La Taberna de Dolores	14
La Tapería del Prado	19

CAFÉ	
Café el Botánico	16

MUSEO REINA SOFÍA

🚇 Atocha 🌐 museoreinasofia.es. Mon & Wed–Sat 10am–9pm, Sun 10am–7pm. €8, free Mon, Wed–Sat 7–9pm, Sun after 1.30pm and for under-18s and over-65s. MAP PP.68–69, POCKET MAP G8

An essential stop on the Madrid art circuit is the Museo Reina Sofía, an immense exhibition space providing a permanent home for the Spanish collection of modern and contemporary art, including the Miró and Picasso legacies.

If the queues at the main entrance are too long, try the alternative one in the extension on the Ronda de Atocha.

As well as its collection of twentieth-century art, the museum has a theatre, cinema, excellent bookshops, a print, music and photographic library, a restaurant, bar and café in the basement and a peaceful inner courtyard garden. An informative, but expensive, guidebook examining some of the key works is available from the shops, priced €22. At the entrance, there are audio-guides in English (€4), which provide informative commentaries for the first-time visitor.

The **permanent collection** begins on the second floor with a section examining the origins of modern Spanish art, largely through the two artistic nuclei that developed in Catalunya and the Basque Country at the end of the nineteenth century.

Midway round Collection 1 is the Reina Sofía's main draw – Picasso's *Guernica* (see box opposite), an emblematic piece that has always evoked strong reactions. Strong sections on Cubism – in the first of which Picasso is again well represented – and the Paris School follow. Dalí and Miró make heavy-weight contributions too in the Surrealism section. The development of Dalí's work and his variety of techniques are clearly displayed, with pieces ranging from the classic *Muchacha en la Ventana* to famous Surrealist works such as *El Enigma de Hitler*. Impressive works from the Cubist Juan Gris are intermingled with a fascinating collection of Spanish sculpture to complete the circuit on this floor.

Collection 2 continues on the fourth floor, although here it's no match for the attractions of the previous exhibits. This section covers Spain's postwar years up to 1968 and includes Spanish and international examples of abstract and avant-garde movements such as Pop Art, Constructivism and Minimalism, one of the highlights being Francis Bacon's *Figura Tumbada* (*Reclining Figure*). Worth hunting out is the section on photography during the years of Franco's dictatorship, and the work by British artists Henry Moore and Graham Sutherland. There are also some striking pieces by the Basque abstract sculptor Chillida and Catalan Surrealist painter Antoni Tàpies.

Jean Nouvel's 79 million-euro state-of-the-art extension, known as the **Area Nouvel**, is built around an open courtyard topped by a striking delta-shaped, metallic, crimson-

---

If you plan to visit all three art museums on the Paseo del Prado during your stay, it's well worth buying the **Paseo del Arte ticket** (€25.60), which is valid for a year and allows one visit to each museum at a substantial saving although it does not include the temporary exhibitions. It's available at any of the three museums.

CENTRO DE ARTE REINA SOFIA

coloured roof. It now houses the third part of the collection covering the period 1962–82, with a focus on experimental, revolutionary and feminist art, dealing with themes from the final years of the Franco dictatorship to the present day. The new wing is also home to temporary exhibition spaces, an auditorium, library, bookshop and café-restaurant.

Guernica

Superbly displayed and no longer protected by the bulletproof glass and steel girders that once imprisoned it, Picasso's *Guernica* is a monumental icon of twentieth-century Spanish art and politics which, despite its familiarity, still has the ability to shock. Picasso painted it in response to the bombing of the Basque town of Gernika in April 1937 by the German Luftwaffe, acting in concert with Franco, during the Spanish Civil War. In the preliminary studies, displayed around the room, you can see how he developed its symbols – the dying horse, the woman mourning, the bull and so on – and then return to the painting to marvel at how he made it all work. Picasso determined that the work be "loaned" to the Museum of Modern Art in New York while Franco remained in power, meaning that the artist never lived to see it displayed in his home country – it only returned to Spain in 1981, eight years after Picasso's death and six after the demise of Franco.

PASEO DEL ARTE AND RETIRO

MUSEO THYSSEN-BORNEMISZA

Ⓜ Banco de España Ⓦ museothyssen.org. Mon noon–4pm, Tues–Sun 10am–7pm. €10 for permanent collection, €9–11 for temporary exhibitions, combined ticket €13–17, permanent collection free Mon. MAP PP.68–69, POCKET MAP H12

This fabulous private collection, assembled by Baron Heinrich Thyssen-Bornemisza, his son Hans Heinrich and his former beauty-queen wife Carmen was first displayed here in 1993 and contains pieces by almost every major Western artist since the fourteenth century.

An extension, built on the site of an adjoining mansion and cleverly integrated into the original format of the museum, houses temporary exhibitions and Carmen's collection, which is particularly strong on nineteenth-century landscape, North American, Impressionist and Post-Impressionist work.

To follow the collection chronologically, begin on the second floor with pre-Renaissance work from the fourteenth century. This is followed by a wonderful array of Renaissance portraits by, amongst others, Ghirlandaio, Raphael and Holbein, including the latter's commanding *Henry VIII*. Beyond are some equally impressive pieces by Titian, Tintoretto, El Greco, Caravaggio and Canaletto, while a superb collection of landscapes and some soothing Impressionist works by Pissarro, Monet, Renoir, Degas and Sisley are housed in the new galleries.

The first floor continues with an outstanding selection of work by Gauguin and the Post-Impressionists. There's excellent coverage, too, of the vivid Expressionist work of Kandinsky, Nolde and Kirchner.

Beyond, the displays include a comprehensive round of seventeenth-century Dutch painting of various genres and some splendid nineteenth-century American landscapes. There are strong contributions from Van Gogh – most notably one of his last and most gorgeous works, *Les Vessenots* – and more from the Expressionists, including the apocalyptic *Metropolis* by George Grosz.

The ground floor covers the period from the beginning of the twentieth century with some outstanding Cubist work from Picasso, Braque and Mondrian to be found within the "experimental avant-garde" section. There are also some marvellous pieces by Miró, Pollock and Chagall. Surrealism is, not surprisingly, represented by Dalí, while the final galleries include some eye-catching work by Bacon, Lichtenstein and Freud.

PARQUE DEL RETIRO

Ⓜ Retiro, Ibiza, Atocha Renfe, Atocha or Banco de España. MAP PP.68–69, POCKET MAP J4–K7

The origins of the wonderful Parque del Retiro (Retiro Park) go back to the early seventeenth century when Felipe IV produced a plan for a new palace and French-style gardens, the Buen Retiro. Of the buildings, only the ballroom

(Casón del Buen Retiro) and the Hall of Realms (the Salón de Reinos) remain.

The park's 330-acre expanse offers the chance to jog, rollerblade, cycle, picnic, row on the lake, have your fortune told, and – above all – **promenade**. The busiest day is Sunday, when half of Madrid turns out for the *paseo*.

Promenading aside, there's almost always something going on in the park, including concerts in the Quiosco de Música, performances by groups of South American pan-piping musicians by the lake and, on summer weekends, puppet shows by the Puerta de Alcalá entrance.

Travelling art exhibitions are frequently housed in the graceful **Palacio de Velázquez** (daily: April–Sept 10am–10pm; Oct–March 10am–6pm; free) and the splendid **Palacio de Cristal** (same hours during exhibitions, but closed when raining; free), while the **Teatro Casa de Vacas** (usually daily 10am–9pm) hosts shows, concerts and plays. Look out,

too, for the magnificently ostentatious statue to Alfonso XII by the lake and the Ángel Caído, supposedly the world's only public statue to Lucifer, in the south of the park. The Bosque de los Ausentes, 192 olive trees and cypresses planted by the Paseo de la Chopera in memory of the victims who died in the train bombings at the nearby Atocha station on March 11, 2004, is close by.

PUERTA DE ALCALÁ

Ⓜ Retiro or Banco de España. MAP PP.68–69, POCKET MAP J4

The Puerta de Alcalá is one of Madrid's most emblematic landmarks. Built in Neoclassical style in 1769 by Francesco Sabatini to commemorate Carlos III's first twenty years on the throne, it was the biggest city gate in Europe at the time. Once on the site of the city's easternmost boundary, it's now marooned on a small island on the traffic-choked Plaza de la Independencia.

JARDÍNES BOTÁNICOS

Plaza de Murillo 2 Ⓜ Atocha Ⓦ www.rjb.csic .es. Daily 10am–dusk. €3, under-10s free. MAP PP.68–69, POCKET MAP H7

The delightful botanical gardens were opened in 1781 by Carlos III. The king's aim was to collect and grow species from all over his Spanish Empire, develop a research centre, and supply medicinal herbs and plants to Madrid's hospitals. Abandoned for much of the last century, they were restored in the 1980s and are now home to some 30,000 species from around the globe. Don't miss the hothouse with its amazing cacti or the bonsai collection of former prime minister Felipe González. Temporary exhibitions take place in the Pabellón Villanueva within the grounds.

PARQUE DEL RETIRO

CAIXAFORUM MADRID

Paseo del Prado 36 Ⓜ Atocha Ⓦ obrasocial
.lacaixa.es. Daily 10am–8pm. €4. MAP PP.68–69,
POCKET MAP H7

An innovative exhibition
space, opened in 2008 by the
Catalan savings bank, which
complements the existing
attractions on the Paseo del
Arte. The centre, which hosts a
variety of high-quality art
shows, is flanked by an
eye-catching **vertical garden**
designed by French botanist
Patrick Blanc in which some
15,000 plants form an organic
carpet extending across the
wall. There is a decent art
bookshop inside, as well.

MUSEO DE ARTES DECORATIVAS

C/Montalbán 12 Ⓜ Banco de España
Ⓦ mnartesdecorativas.mcu.es. Tues–Sat
9.30am–3pm, Sun 10am–3pm, plus Thurs
5–8pm Sept–June. €3, free on Sun and Thurs
eve. MAP PP.68–69, POCKET MAP J5

The national collection of
decorative arts is housed in an
elegant nineteenth-century
mansion. The highlight is its
collection of *azulejos* (tiles)
and other ceramics with a
magnificent eighteenth-
century tiled Valencian
kitchen on the top floor. The
rest of the exhibits include an
interesting but unspectacular
collection of furniture, a series
of reconstructed rooms and
objets d'art from all over Spain.

MUSEO NAVAL

Paseo del Prado 5 Ⓜ Banco de España
Ⓦ armada.mde.es. Tues–Sun 10am–7pm;
closed public hols. Free (bring ID; voluntary €3
donation requested). MAP PP.68–69, POCKET MAP J11

As you might expect, the Naval
Museum is strong on models,
charts and navigational aids
relating to Spanish voyages of
discovery. Exhibits include the
first map to show the New
World, drawn in 1500 by Juan
de la Cosa, cannons from the
Spanish Armada and part of
Cortés' standard used during the
conquest of Mexico. The room
dedicated to the *Nao San Diego*,
sunk during a conflict with the
Dutch off the Philippines in
1600, contains fascinating items
recovered during the salvage
operation in the early 1990s.

SAN JERÓNIMO EL REAL

C/Ruiz de Alarcón 19 Ⓜ Atocha or Banco de
España. Sept–June: Mon–Sat 10am–1pm &
5–8.30pm, Sun & hols 9.30am–2.30pm &
5.30–8.30pm; July & Aug: Mon–Sat 10am–1pm
& 6–8.30pm, Sun & hols 9.30am–1.30pm &
6–8.30pm. MAP PP.68–69, POCKET MAP H6

Madrid's high-society church
was built on the site of a
monastery founded in the early

MUSEO DE ARTES DECORATIVAS

sixteenth century by the Catholic monarchs, Fernando and Isabel. It later became the venue for the swearing-in of the heirs to the throne and setting for many royal marriages and coronations (including the former king, Juan Carlos, in 1975). Despite remodelling and the addition of two Gothic towers, the old form of the church is still visible; but the seventeenth-century cloisters have fallen victim to the Prado extension.

MONUMENTO A LOS CAÍDOS POR ESPAÑA

PLAZA DE LA LEALTAD (MONUMENTO A LOS CAÍDOS POR ESPAÑA)

Ⓜ Banco de España. MAP PP.68–69, POCKET MAP H6
This aristocratic plaza contains the **Monument to Spain's Fallen**. Originally a memorial to the *Madrileños* who died in the 1808 anti-French rebellion (the urn at the base contains their ashes), it was later changed to commemorate all those who have died fighting for Spain, and an eternal flame now burns here. On one side of the plaza stands the opulent *Ritz Hotel*, work of Charles Mewès, architect of the *Ritz* hotels in Paris and London, while opposite is the Madrid stock exchange.

ESTACIÓN DE ATOCHA

Ⓜ Atocha or Atocha Renfe. MAP PP.68–69, POCKET MAP J8
The grand Estación de Atocha is now sadly infamous as the scene of the horrific train bombings that killed 191 people and injured close to 2000 in March 2004. A glass memorial to the victims stands just outside one of the entrances on Paseo de la Infanta Isabel. The tower channels light into an underground chamber (access via the station) lined with an inner membrane on which are written messages of condolence. The old station alongside was revamped in 1992 and is a glorious 1880s glasshouse, resembling a tropical garden. It's a wonderful sight from the walkways above, as a constant spray of water rains down on the jungle of vegetation. At the platforms beyond sit the gleaming AVE trains.

MUSEO NACIONAL DE ANTROPOLOGÍA/ETNOLOGÍA

C/Alfonso XII 68 Ⓜ Atocha or Atocha Renfe Ⓦ mnantropologia.mcu.es. Tues–Sat 9.30am–8pm, Sun 10am–3pm. €3, free Sat after 2pm & Sun. MAP PP.68–69, POCKET MAP J8
The National Anthropology and Ethnography Museum was founded by the eccentric Dr Pedro González Velasco to house his private collection. The displays give an overview of different cultures, particularly those linked to Spanish history. The most interesting exhibits include a macabre collection of deformed skulls, a Guanche mummy (the original inhabitants of the Canary Islands), some shrivelled embryos and the skeleton of a 2.35m tall circus giant, which Velasco had agreed to buy from the owner after his death – payment in advance of course.

REAL FÁBRICA DE TAPICES

C/Fuentarrabía 2 Ⓜ Atocha Renfe or
Menéndez Pelayo ⓦrealfabricadetapices
.com. Mon–Fri 10am–2pm; closed Aug &
Dec 24–Jan 2. €4. Tours every half-hour.
MAP PP.68-69, POCKET MAP K9

The Royal Tapestry Workshop
makes for a fascinating visit.
Founded in 1721 and moved to
its present site in the
nineteenth century, the factory
uses processes and machines
unchanged for hundreds of
years. The handful of workers
that remain can be seen coolly
looping handfuls of bobbins
around myriad strings and
sewing up worn-out masterpieces with exactly matching
silk. With progress painfully
slow – one worker produces a
square metre of tapestry every
three and a half months – the
astronomical prices soon seem
easily understandable.

Shops

CUESTA MOYANO

Cuesta de Claudio Moyano Ⓜ Atocha.
MAP PP.68-69, POCKET MAP H8

A row of little wooden kiosks
on a hill close to the Retiro
selling just about every book
you could think of, from
second-hand copies of Captain
Marvel to Cervantes. Other
items include old prints of
Madrid and relics from the
Franco era.

OBJETOS DE ARTE TOLEDANO

Paseo del Prado 10 Ⓜ Atocha or Banco de
España. Mon–Sat 10am–8pm. MAP PP.68-69,
POCKET MAP H13

Souvenir shop stocking "typical
Spanish"-style goods including
fans, Lladró porcelain, T-shirts
and tacky flamenco accessories,
as well as more unlikely gifts like
armour and Toledan swords.

PIEL DE TORO

Paseo del Prado 42 Ⓜ Atocha or Banco de
España ⓦ pieldetoro.com. Daily 10am–8pm.
MAP PP.68-69, POCKET MAP H7

A colourful range of expensive
T-shirts, sweatshirts, jerseys and
baseball caps, all emblazoned
with the emblem of a bull.
Despite the clichéd image, they
make good, lightweight presents.

Café

CAFÉ EL BOTÁNICO

C/Ruiz de Alarcón 27 Ⓜ Atocha or Banco de
España ⓦ restaurantebotanico.com. Mon–Thurs
9am–11pm, Fri & Sat 9am–12.30am, Sun
9am–7pm. MAP PP.68-69, POCKET MAP H7

Ideal for a refreshing drink
after visiting the Prado; this

well-established café/bar sits in a quiet street by the botanical gardens and serves good beer and a small selection of tapas. Service can be slow.

Restaurants

ÁLBORA

C/Jorge Juan 33 ⓜ Velázquez or Príncipe de Vergara ☎ 917 816 197, ⓦ restaurantealbora .com. Mon–Sat 1.30–4pm & 8.30pm–midnight, Sun 1.30–4pm. MAP PP.68–69, POCKET MAP K3

A Michelin-star restaurant run by renowned chef David Garcia serving exquisite contemporary Spanish cuisine based on seasonal products. There are taster menus at €55 and €74 per head, and there is the option to sample some more reasonably priced offerings such as roast octopus and cod tortilla at the bar.

EL BUEY

C/General Diaz Porlier 9 ⓜ Goya ☎ 915 758 066, ⓦ restauranteelbuey.com. Mon–Sat 1–4pm & 9pm–midnight, Sun 1–4pm. MAP PP.68–69, POCKET MAP K3

Top-quality meat accompanied by an excellent array of starters, side dishes and salads in this friendly little restaurant near the Retiro. Prices – €35 a head – are reasonable considering the quality, and there is a very good three-course set menu with a decent house red for under €40.

CASA PORTAL

C/Dr Castelo 26 ⓜ Ibiza ☎ 915 742 026, ⓦ casa-portal.com. Tues & Sun 1.30–4pm, Wed–Sat 1.30–4pm & 8.30–11.30pm. Closed hols & Aug. MAP PP.68–69, POCKET MAP K4

Despite a change of ownership, *Casa Portal* retains its reputation for superlative Asturian cooking – go for the *fabada* (beans, chorizo and black pudding stew) or *besugo* (bream), washed down with some cider. The shellfish is

excellent too. Around €35–40 per person.

EDELWEISS

C/Jovellanos 7 ⓜ Banco de España ☎ 915 323 383. 1–4pm & 8pm–midnight. Closed Sun eve. MAP PP.68–69, POCKET MAP G11

Renowned German restaurant with an array of central European specialities and large portions. Expect to pay around €35 a head, although there's a €20 lunchtime menu including *Bratwurst*.

EL MIRADOR DEL MUSEO THYSSEN

Paseo del Prado 8 ⓜ Banco de España ☎ 914 293 984. Tues–Sat 8.30pm–2.30am July & Aug only. MAP PP.68–69, POCKET MAP H12

Summer-only terrace restaurant on the top floor of the art museum with some great views over the city. Specializes in Mediterranean cuisine; dishes include smoked salmon with pear paté. Reservations essential; €40–50 a head.

LA MONTERÍA

C/Lope de Rueda 35 ⓜ Ibiza ☎ 915 741 812, ⓦ lamonteria.es. Mon–Sat 2–4pm & 8.30pm–11pm. MAP PP.68–69, POCKET MAP K4

This inconspicuous little restaurant on the Retiro's eastern edge was recently revamped, and serves some of the tastiest food in the area. The speciality *salmorejo* is excellent, as are the battered prawns, while mains include partridge and monkfish options. At least €35 a head.

AL MOUNIA

C/Recoletos 5 ⓜ Banco de España ☎ 914 350 828, ⓦ restaurantealmounia.es. Tues–Sat 1.30–4pm & 9–11.30pm, Sun 1.30–4pm. Closed Aug. MAP PP.68–69, POCKET MAP H4

Moroccan cooking at its best in the most established Arabic restaurant in town. The couscous, lamb and desserts are a must. Mains cost over €20; lunchtime menus start at €32.

VIRIDIANA

PARADÍS MADRID

C/Marqués de Cubas 14 Ⓜ Banco de
España ☎ 914 297 303, Ⓦ restaurante
paradismadrid.es. Mon–Sat 1.30–4pm &
9pm–midnight, Sun 9pm–midnight. MAP
PP.68-69, POCKET MAP H12

Upmarket Catalan restaurant
frequented by politicians from
the nearby parliament. High-
quality Mediterranean food
with superb starters, fish and
rice dishes; the *fideuà* with
duck's liver and boletus
mushrooms is a stand out..
Menus from €25.

TABERNA LAREDO

C/Dr Castelo 30 Ⓜ Ibiza ☎ 915 733 061,
Ⓦ tabernalaredo.com. Mon–Sat noon–midnight.
Closed Aug. MAP PP.68-69, POCKET MAP K4

Delicious salads, risottos and
fish dishes served up with style
at this acclaimed bar/restaurant
close to the Retiro. The €42
sampler menu is a very good
option. Reservations essential.

TABERNA PEDRAZA

C/Ibiza 40 Ⓜ Ibiza ☎ 910 327 200,
Ⓦ tabernapedraza.com. Tues–Sun 1–4.30pm
& 8–11.30pm. MAP PP.68-69, POCKET MAP K4

Well-regarded gastrobar just
to the east of the Retiro, run

by a married couple. Excellent
tortilla and *croquetas*, as well
as a seasonal selection of
dishes from around Spain.
Expect to pay around €35 per
head for an evening meal.

LA VERÓNICA

C/Moratín 38 Ⓜ Antón Martín ☎ 914 297
827, Ⓦ restaurantelaveronica.com. Mon–Sat
1–4.30pm & 8.30pm–12.30am, Sun 1–4.30pm.
MAP P.68-69, POCKET MAP H14

A wide range of dishes at this
slightly bohemian little restaurant. Try the *carne* or the
carabinero con pasta (pasta
with red prawns), which have
been staple dishes at the
restaurant for the last 25
years.. Lunchtime menus at
€11 and €16.

VIRIDIANA

C/Juan de Mena 14 Ⓜ Banco de España
☎ 915 311 039, Ⓦ restauranteviridiana.com.
Daily 1.30–4pm & 8.30pm–midnight. Closed
Easter & Aug. MAP PP.68-69, POCKET MAP J5

A bizarre temple of Madrid
nueva cocina (new cuisine),
decorated with photos from
Luis Buñuel's film of the same
name and offering mouth-
watering creations, plus a
superb selection of wines.
The bill for a three-course
meal is likely to come close
to €100 a head but it's an
unforgettable experience.

Tapas bars

CERVECERÍA CERVANTES

Plaza de Jesús 7 Ⓜ Antón Martín or Banco de
España. Mon–Sat 12.30–5pm & 7.30–11.45pm,
Sun noon–4pm. MAP PP.68-69, POCKET MAP H13

Great beer and excellent fresh
seafood tapas in this busy
little bar just behind the
Palace Hotel. The *gambas*
(prawns) go down a treat with
a cool glass of the beer, while
the *tosta de gambas* (a sort of
prawn toast) is a must.

LA FÁBRICA

Plaza de Jesús 2 Ⓜ Antón Martín or Banco de España. Mon–Thurs 9.30–12.30am, Fri & Sat 11am–2am, Sun 10am–5pm. MAP PP.68–69, POCKET MAP H13

Bustling, friendly bar serving a delicious range of canapés – the smoked cod is one of the favourites – plus chilled beer and good vermouth.

LA PLATERÍA

C/Moratín 49 Ⓜ Antón Martín or Atocha. Mon–Fri 7.30am–1am, Sat & Sun 9.30am–1am. MAP PP.68–69, POCKET MAP H14

This bar has a popular summer terraza geared to a tourist clientele and a good selection of reasonably priced tapas available all day. Service can be a little brusque though.

LA TABERNA DE DOLORES

Plaza de Jesús 4 Ⓜ Antón Martín or Banco de España. Daily 11am–midnight. MAP PP.68–69, POCKET MAP H13

A standing-room-only tiled bar, decorated with beer bottles from around the world. The beer is great and the splendid food specialities include roquefort and anchovy and smoked-salmon canapés.

LA TAPERÍA DEL PRADO

Plaza Platerías de Martínez 1 Ⓜ Antón Martín or Banco de España ☎ 914 294 094, Ⓦ lataperia.es. Mon–Thurs 8am–1am, Fri–Sun 10am–2am. MAP PP.68–69, POCKET MAP J14

Modern bar serving up a range of tapas and raciones, as well as breakfasts and afternoon snacks. Portions are on the small side.

Bar

LE CABRERA

C/Bárbara de Braganza 2 Ⓜ Colón Ⓦ lecabrera .com. Wed, Thurs & Sun 7pm–2am, Fri & Sat 7pm–2.30am. MAP PP.68–69, POCKET MAP H3

A chic bar serving drinks and mouth-watering creative tapas

in the gastro bar on the ground floor and expertly mixed cocktails in the cosier basement area. There's another branch in the Casa de América at Paseo de Recoletos 2.

Clubs

ALEGORÍA/ALQUIMIA

C/Villanueva 2 (entrance on C/Cid) Ⓜ Colón ☎ 915 772 785, Ⓦ alegoriamadrid. com. Thurs 8pm–4am, Fri 9pm–5.30am, Sat 9.30pm–6am, Sun 7pm–12.30am. Entrance €10, free Thurs & Sun. MAP PP.68–69, POCKET MAP J3

Modelled on an English gentleman's club, this restaurant, bar and disco comes complete with leather sofas, a wood-panelled library, Gothic statuary and models of old sailing ships hanging from the ceiling.

KAPITAL

C/Atocha 125 Ⓜ Atocha Ⓦ grupo-kapital.com /kapital. Thurs–Sat midnight–6am. €17 with two drinks. MAP PP.68–69, POCKET MAP H8

A seven-floor club catering for practically every taste, with three dancefloors, lasers, go-go dancers, a cinema and a terraza. The eclectic musical menu features disco, house, merengue, salsa, sevillanas and even the occasional session of karaoke.

ALEGORÍA

Gran Vía, Chueca and Malasaña

The Gran Vía, one of Madrid's main thoroughfares, effectively divides the old city to the south from the newer parts in the north. Heaving with traffic, shoppers and sightseers, it's the commercial heart of the city, and a monument in its own right, with its turn-of-the-twentieth-century, palace-like banks and offices. North of here, and bursting with bars, restaurants and nightlife, are two of the city's most vibrant *barrios*: Chueca, focal point of Madrid's gay scene, and Malasaña, former centre of the Movida Madrileña, the happening scene of the late 1970s and early 1980s, and still a somewhat alternative area, focusing on lively Plaza Dos de Mayo. As well as the bustling atmosphere, a couple of museums and a number of beautiful churches in the area provide even more reasons for a visit.

GRAN VÍA

Ⓜ Gran Vía. MAP PP.82–83, POCKET MAP D10–G10

The Gran Vía (Great Way), built in three stages at the start of the twentieth century, became a symbol of Spain's arrival in the modern world. Financed on the back of an economic boom, experienced as a result of the country's neutrality in World War I, the Gran Vía is a showcase for a whole gamut of architectural styles, from Modernist to Neo-Rococo.

The finest section is the earliest, constructed between 1910 and 1924 and stretching from C/Alcalá to the Telefónica skyscraper. Particularly noteworthy are the Edificio Metrópolis (1905–11), complete with cylindrical facade, white

GRAN VÍA

stone sculptures, zinc-tiled roof and gold garlands, and the nearby Grassy building (1916–17). The vast 81m-high slab of the Telefónica building was Spain's first skyscraper. During the Civil War it was used as a reference point by Franco's forces to bomb the area. The stretch down to Plaza de Callao is dominated by shops, cafés and cinemas, while the plaza itself is now the gateway to the shoppers' haven of C/Preciados. On the corner is the classic Art Deco Capitol building (1930–33), its curved facade embellished with lurid neon signs. Cast your eyes skywards on the final stretch downhill towards Plaza de España to catch sight of an assortment of statues and decorations that top many of the buildings.

PLAZA DE CHUECA

PLAZA DE CHUECA

Ⓜ Chueca. MAP PP.82–83, POCKET MAP G3

The smaller streets north of Gran Vía, although still home to some vice-related activities, are gradually being spruced up. Further north in Plaza de Chueca, there's a strong neighbourhood feel and a lively gay scene at night. The area has been rejuvenated in recent years and now holds some enticing streets lined with offbeat restaurants, small private art galleries and unusual corner shops. Calle Almirante has some of the city's most fashionable clothes shops and Calle Augusto Figueroa is the place to go for shoes.

LAS SALESAS REALES

Plaza de las Salesas Ⓜ Colon. Mon–Fri 9am–1pm & 6–9pm, Sat 10am–1pm & 6–9pm, Sun 10am–2pm & 6–9pm. MAP PP.82–83, POCKET MAP H3

The Santa Bárbara church was originally part of the convent complex of Las Salesas Reales, founded in 1747. The church is

set behind a fine forecourt, while inside, there's a grotto-like chapel, delightful frescoes and stained-glass windows, and some striking green marble altar decoration. The tombs of Fernando VI, his wife Bárbara de Bragança and military hero General O'Donnell lie within.

SOCIEDAD DE AUTORES

C/Fernando VI 4 Ⓜ Alonso Martinez.
MAP PP.82–83, POCKET MAP G3

Home to the Society of Authors, this is the most significant Modernista building in Madrid. Designed in 1902 by the Catalan architect José Grasés Riera, its facade features a dripping decoration of flowers, faces and balconies.

PLAZA DEL DOS DE MAYO

Ⓜ Tribunal or Bilbao. MAP PP.82–83, POCKET MAP E2

Plaza del Dos de Mayo is the centre of a lively bar scene, with people spilling onto the streets that converge on the square. The plaza commemorates the rebellion against occupying French troops in 1808, while the neighbourhood gets its name from a young seamstress, Manuela Malasaña, who became one of the rebellion's heroines.

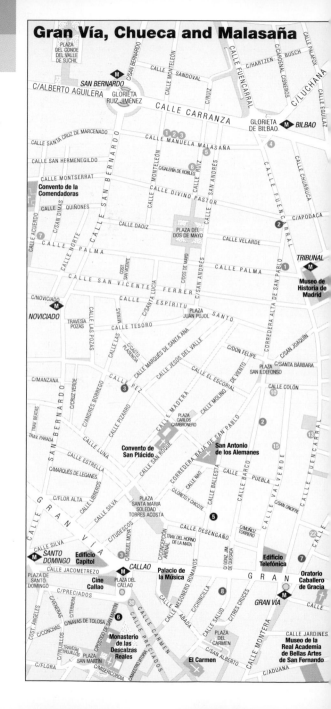

Gran Vía, Chueca and Malasaña

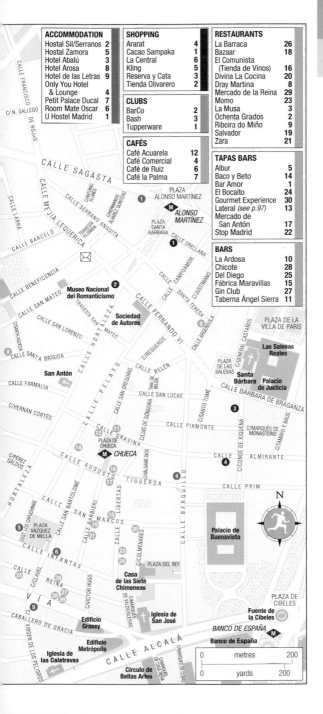

ACCOMMODATION

Hostal Sil/Serranos	2
Hostal Zamora	5
Hotel Abalú	3
Hotel Arosa	8
Hotel de las Letras	9
Only You Hotel & Lounge	4
Petit Palace Ducal	7
Room Mate Oscar	6
U Hostel Madrid	1

SHOPPING

Ararat	4
Cacao Sampaka	1
La Central	6
Kling	5
Reserva y Cata	3
Tienda Olivarero	2

CLUBS

BarCo	2
Bash	3
Tupperware	1

CAFÉS

Café Acuarela	12
Café Comercial	4
Café de Ruiz	7
Café la Palma	6

RESTAURANTS

La Barraca	26
Bazaar	18
El Comunista (Tienda de Vinos)	16
Divina La Cocina	20
Dray Martina	8
Mercado de la Reina	29
Momo	23
La Musa	3
Ochenta Grados	2
Ribeira do Miño	9
Salvador	19
Zara	21

TAPAS BARS

Albur	5
Baco y Beto	14
Bar Amor	1
El Bocaito	24
Gourmet Experience	30
Lateral (see p.97)	13
Mercado de San Antón	17
Stop Madrid	22

BARS

La Ardosa	10
Chicote	28
Del Diego	25
Fábrica Maravillas	15
Gin Club	27
Taberna Ángel Sierra	11

MUSEO NACIONAL DEL ROMANTICISMO

C/San Mateo 13 Ⓜ Tribunal
Ⓦ museoromanticismo.mcu.es. May–Oct
Tues–Sat 9.30am–8.30pm (closes 6.30pm
Nov–April), Sun 10am–3pm. €3, free on Sat
after 2pm, Sun. MAP PP.82–83, POCKET MAP F2

The Museo del Romanticismo
aims to show the lifestyle and
outlook of the late-Romantic
era through the re-creation of a
typical bourgeois residence in
the turbulent reign of Isabel II
(1833–68), and this it does
brilliantly. Overflowing with a
marvellously eclectic and often
kitsch hoard of memorabilia,
the mansion is decorated with
some stunning period furniture
and ceiling frescoes, together
with more bizarre exhibits such
as the pistol which the satirist
Mariano José de Larra used to
shoot himself in 1837 after
being spurned by his lover.

MUSEO DE HISTORIA DE MADRID

C/Fuencarral 78 Ⓜ Tribunal Ⓦ www.madrid.es
/museodehistoria. Tues–Fri 11am–2pm &
4–7pm, Sat & Sun 10am–2pm & 4–7pm. Free.
MAP PP.82–83, POCKET MAP F2

Just around the corner from the
Museo del Romanticismo, the
Museo de Historia de Madrid
has now been fully reopened
after a lengthy restoration
programme. The former city

almshouse was remodelled in
the early eighteenth century by
Pedro de Ribera and features
one of his trademark elaborately
decorated Baroque doorways
superimposed on a striking red
brick facade. Inside, the
museum contains an intriguing
collection of paintings, photos,
models, sculptures and porcelain, all relating to the history
and urban development of
Madrid since 1561 (the date it
was designated imperial capital
by Felipe II). One of the star
exhibits is a fascinating 3-D
model of the city made in 1830
by military engineer León Gil
de Palacio.

SAN ANTONIO DE LOS ALEMANES

Corredera de San Pablo 16 Ⓜ Chueca or
Callao. Mon–Sat 10.30am–2pm. Closed Aug.
€2. MAP PP.82–83, POCKET MAP E3

Opening hours are limited,
coinciding with Mass, but this
little church – designed in 1624
by the Jesuit architect Pedro
Sánchez and Juan Gómez de
Mora – is one of the city's
hidden treasures. The elliptical
interior is lined with dizzying
floor-to-ceiling pastel-coloured
frescoes by Neapolitan artist
Luca Giordano which depict
scenes from the life of
St Anthony.

SAN ANTONIO DE LOS ALEMANES

LA CENTRAL

Shops

ARARAT

C/Almirante 10 Ⓜ Chueca. Mon–Sat 11am–2pm & 5–8.30pm. MAP PP.82–83, POCKET MAP G3

Spanish and foreign designers for women, often at reduced prices. You can find formal and party wear, as well as younger styles.

CACAO SAMPAKA

C/Orellana 4 Ⓜ Alonso Martinez Ⓦ cacaosampaka.com. Mon–Sat 10am–9pm; closed Aug. MAP PP.82–83, POCKET MAP G2

There's every conceivable shape, colour and flavour of chocolate here, ranging from rose and strawberry to gin and tonic. The only surprise is that their restaurant menu has some non-chocolate options.

LA CENTRAL

C/Postigo de San Martín 8 Ⓜ Callao Ⓦ lacentral.com. Mon–Fri 9.30am–10pm, Sat 10am–10pm, Sun 10am–9.30pm. MAP PP.82–83, POCKET MAP C10

Stunning bookshop over four floors of a beautifully decorated building just off Plaza Callao. As well as thumbing through copies of its comprehensive selection of Spanish, Latin American and English classics, you can admire the frescoed ceilings, check out the basement cocktail bar or have a drink in the café.

KLING

C/Ballesta 6 Ⓜ Gran Vía Ⓦ kling.es. Mon–Thurs 9.30am–2pm & 3.30–6pm, Fri 9am–2.30pm. MAP PP.82–83, POCKET MAP E4

Fun, young fashion for women at good prices in this popular store, located in an up-and-coming area north of Gran Vía that is trying to throw off its reputation as a red light area.

RESERVA Y CATA

C/Conde de Xiquena 13 Ⓜ Chueca Ⓦ reservaycata.com. Mon 5–9pm, Tues–Fri 11am–3pm & 5–9pm, Sat 11am–3pm. MAP PP.82–83, POCKET MAP G3

Staff at this friendly shop help you select from some of the best new wines in the Iberian peninsula, and run wine tastings too.

TIENDA OLIVARERO

C/Mejia Lequerica 1 Ⓜ Alonso Martinez. Sept–June Mon–Fri 10am–2pm & 5–8pm, Sat 10am–2pm; July 10am–3pm. Closed Aug. MAP PP.82–83, POCKET MAP G2

This olive-growers' co-operative outlet has useful information sheets to help you buy the best olive oils from around Spain.

Cafés

CAFÉ ACUARELA

C/Gravina 10 Ⓜ Chueca. Daily 2pm–2am. MAP PP.82–83, POCKET MAP G3

Comfy café with over-the-top Baroque decor and great cocktails, popular with a mostly LGBT crowd.

CAFÉ DE RUIZ

C/Ruiz 11 Ⓜ Bilbao Ⓦ cafederuiz.com.
Mon–Sat 3.30pm–2am, Sun 3.30–11.30pm.
MAP PP.82–83, POCKET MAP E2

Classic Malasaña café and a
great place to while away an
afternoon. Discreet background
music and good cakes are
followed by cocktails in the
evening.

CAFÉ LA PALMA

C/Palma 62 Ⓜ Noviciado Ⓦ cafelapalma.
com. Daily 4pm–3am. MAP PP.82–83, POCKET MAP
D2

Part traditional café, part arts
and music venue, *Café La
Palma* acts as a stage for a
myriad of local artists ranging
from singer-songwriters to
storytellers. It also has popular
DJ sessions on many evenings,
as well as holding regular open
mic nights.

Restaurants

LA BARRACA

C/Reina 29 Ⓜ Bilbao ☎ 915 327 154.
Ⓦ labarraca.es. Daily 1.30–4.15pm & 8pm–
midnight. MAP PP.82–83, POCKET MAP F10

Step off the dingy street into
this little piece of Valencia for
some of the best paella in town.
The starters are excellent and
there's a great lemon sorbet for
dessert too. A three-course
meal with wine costs around
€35 a head.

BAZAAR

C/Libertad 21 Ⓜ Chueca. Mon–Wed & Sun
1.15–4pm & 8.30–11.30pm, Thurs–Sat
1.15–4pm & 8.15pm–midnight. MAP PP.82–83,
POCKET MAP G4

Fusion-style Mediterranean
and Asian cuisine. Lunchtime
menu is €10; evening meals
around €20. The downside is
the production-line-style
service. No reservations, so
arrive early.

EL COMUNISTA (TIENDA DE VINOS)

C/Augusto Figueroa 35 Ⓜ Chueca ☎ 915 217
012. Daily noon–4pm & 8pm–midnight. Closed
mid-Aug to mid-Sept. MAP PP.82–83, POCKET MAP G4

Long-established *comedor* that
has changed little since it was
given its unofficial name as a
student haunt under Franco.
The *sopa de ajo* (garlic soup) is
delicious.

DIVINA LA COCINA

C/Colmenares 13 Ⓜ Chueca ☎ 915 313 765.
Mon–Sun 1–4pm & 9pm–midnight (open till
1am on Sat & Sun). MAP PP.82–83, POCKET MAP G4

Fashionable restaurant on a
little street close to Gran Vía.
Lunch menus from €12.90; the
evening menu is more
expensive (around €26). Dishes
include courgette and duck
terrine and salmon in green
pepper sauce.

DRAY MARTINA

C/Argensola 7 Ⓜ Alonso Martínez ☎ 910 810
056. Ⓦ draymartina.com. Mon–Fri
8.30am–2am, Sat & Sun 10am–2am. MAP
PP.82–83, POCKET MAP G3

This popular new gastrobar is a
café, restaurant and *bar de
copas* all rolled into one. Trendy
vintage-style decor provides the
backdrop, and they serve up a
fresh and imaginative set lunch
for around €12.

MOMO

C/Libertad 8 Ⓜ Chueca ☎ 915 327 348. Daily
1–4pm & 9.30pm–midnight. MAP PP.82–83,
POCKET MAP G4

The place to go for a *menú del
día* with a little bit extra. For
€18 you get three courses, with
options such as salmon with
mango or grilled chicken in
ginger and lemon.

LA MUSA

C/Manuela Malasaña 18 Ⓜ Bilbao ☎ 914
487 558, Ⓦ grupolamusa.com. Mon–Thurs
9am–1am, Fri 9am–2am, Sat 1pm–2am, Sun
1pm–1am. MAP PP.82–83, POCKET MAP E1

A firm favourite on the Malasaña scene. Good tapas, generous helpings, a strong wine list and chic decor are all part of *La Musa's* recipe for success – the only real problem is the crowds.

OCHENTA GRADOS

C/Manuela Malasaña 10 ⓜ Bilbao ☎ 914 458 351, ⓦ ochentagrados.com. Mon–Thurs & Sun 1.30–4pm & 8.30pm–midnight, Fri & Sat 1.30–4.30pm & 8.30pm–2am. MAP PP.82–83, POCKET MP E1

The idea behind *Ochenta Grados* is to serve traditional main course dishes in miniature, and it works wonderfully. Forget the idea of a starter and a main; just order a few dishes to share from the inventive menu, maybe steak tartare with mustard or parmesan ice cream and prawn risotto. Each dish is around €5.

RIBEIRA DO MIÑO

C/Santa Brígida 1 ⓜ Tribunal ☎ 915 219 854, ⓦ marisqueriaribeiradomino.com. Tues–Sun 1–4pm & 8pm–midnight. Closed Aug. MAP PP.82–83, POCKET MAP F3

Great-value *marisquería*, serving fabulous seafood platters and Galician specialities at great prices; try the slightly more expensive Galician white wine, Albariño. Reservations essential.

SALVADOR

C/Barbieri 12 ⓜ Chueca ☎ 915 214 524, ⓦ casasalvadormadrid.com. Mon–Sat 1.30–4pm & 8.30pm–midnight. Closed Aug. MAP PP.82–83, POCKET MAP G4

Chueca mainstay with bullfighting decor and dishes such as *rabo de toro* (bull's tail), stuffed peppers and *arroz con leche* (rice pudding). Lunch around €24.

ZARA

C/Barbieri 8 ⓜ Chueca/Gran Vía ☎ 915 322 074, ⓦ restaurantezara.com. Tues–Sat 1–4.30pm & 8–11.30pm. Closed public hols. MAP PP.82–83, POCKET MAP F4

Excellent food for very good prices at this Cuban restaurant. *Ropa vieja* (strips of beef), fried yucca, minced beef with fried bananas and other specialities; the daiquiris are very good, too. Prices are moderate (under €30).

Tapas bars

ALBUR

C/Manuela Malasaña 15 ⓜ Bilbao ⓦ restaurantealbur.com. Mon–Thurs 12.30–5pm & 7.30pm–midnight, Fri 12.30–5pm & 7.30pm–1.30am, Sat 1pm–1.30am, Sun 1pm–midnight. MAP PP.82–83, POCKET MAP E1

The decor is rustic and the food excellent here. The salads and rice dishes are particularly tasty and the lunchtime menu good value.

LA BARRACA

BACO Y BETO

C/Pelayo 24 ⓜ Chueca ⓦ baco-beto.com.
Mon–Fri 8pm–1am, Sat 2–4.30pm &
8pm–1am. MAP PP.82–83, POCKET MAP F3

Creative tapas in this small bar
in the heart of Chueca. Try the
courgette with melted brie and
the home-made *croquetas*.

BAR AMOR

C/Manuela Malsaña 22 ⓜ San Bernardo or
Bilbao ☎ 915 944 829, ⓦ baramor.es.
Tues–Sat 1.30–4pm & 8pm–midnight.
MAP PP.82–83, POCKET MAP E1

A new arrival on the Malasaña
scene, this compact little corner
restaurant has a carefully
selected menu of appetising
and appealingly presented
raciones – think langoustine
kebabs in rosemary sauce, or
warm salad with Chinese leaves
and scallops. There is a good
wine list, too.

EL BOCAITO

C/Libertad 6 ⓜ Chueca ⓦ bocaito.com.
Mon–Sat 1–4pm & 8.30pm–midnight. Closed
2 weeks in Aug. MAP PP.82–83, POCKET MAP G4

Watch the busy staff preparing
the food in the kitchen as you
munch on delicious tapas. Try
the *Luisito* (chilli, squid and a
secret sauce all topped with a
prawn), the hottest canapé
you're ever likely to encounter.
If you prefer to sit down, there
is a restaurant at the back.

GOURMET EXPERIENCE

El Corte Inglés, Plaza Callao 2 ⓜ Callao.
Mon–Sat 10am–midnight. MAP PP.82–83,
POCKET MAP D10

Head for the ninth floor of this
branch of the classic Spanish
department store to enjoy some
breathtaking views of Madrid.
Gaze out over the Capitol
building on the Gran Vía, the
Palacio Real, and out towards
the distant mountains as you
sample a tapa, some oysters, a
drink or an ice cream from one
of the bars and food stalls set
up on the top floor.

MERCADO DE SAN ANTÓN

C/Augusto Figueroa 24 ⓜ Chueca ⓦ mercado
sananton.com. Mon–Sat 10am–10pm,
terrace & restaurant Mon–Thurs & Sun
10am–midnight, Fri & Sat 10am–1.30am.
MAP PP.82–83, POCKET MAP G4

Like the *Mercado San Miguel*
near Plaza Mayor, this local
market has become a trendy
meeting place on the Chueca
scene with gourmet foodstands,
a wine bar, a café, a sushi stall
and a stylish terrace restaurant.

STOP MADRID

C/Hortaleza 11 ⓜ Gran Vía ⓦ stopmadrid.es.
Daily 12.30pm–2am. MAP PP.82–83, POCKET MAP F4

Dating back to 1929, this
corner bar has hams hanging
from the windows and wine
bottles lining the walls. Tapas
consist largely of *jamón* and
chorizo, and the "Canapé Stop"
of ham and tomato doused in
olive oil is an excellent option.

Bars

LA ARDOSA

C/Colón 13 ⓜ Tribunal ⓦ www.laardosa.com.
Mon–Fri 8.30am–2am, Sat & Sun 11.45am–
2.30am. MAP PP.82–83, POCKET MAP F3

One of the city's classic
tabernas, serving limited but
delicious tapas including great
croquetas, *salmorejo* and an
excellent home-made *tortilla*.
Also draft beer and Guinness.

CHICOTE

Gran Vía 12 ⓜ Gran Vía ⓦ museo-chicote
.com. Mon–Sat 5pm–1.30am. MAP PP.82–83,
POCKET MAP F10

Opened back in 1931 by Perico
Chicote, ex-barman at the *Ritz*.
Sophia Loren, Frank Sinatra,
Ava Gardner, Luis Buñuel,
Orson Welles and Hemingway
have all passed through the
doors of this cocktail bar. It's

lost much of its old-style charm as it has tried to keep up to date, though it's still worth a visit for nostalgia's sake.

DEL DIEGO

C/Reina 12 Ⓜ Gran Vía Ⓦ deldiego.com. Mon–Sat 7.30pm–3am. Closed Aug. MAP PP.82–83, POCKET MAP F10

New York-style cocktail bar set up by former *Chicote* waiter Fernando del Diego and now better than the original place. The expertly mixed cocktails are served up in a friendly, unhurried atmosphere. Margaritas, mojitos and manhattans; the eponymously named vodka-based house special is a must.

FÁBRICA MARAVILLAS

C/Valverde 29 Ⓜ Gran Vía or Tribunal Ⓦ fabricamaravillas.com. Mon–Fri 6pm–midnight, Sat & Sun 12.30pm–midnight. MAP PP.82–83, POCKET MAP F3

Opened in 2012 in this fashionable, rejuvenated street running parallel to C/Fuencarral, Fábrica has helped promote the trend for craft beers in Madrid. An excellent collection of ales, including the fruity Malasaña, stout and an excellent IPA.

GIN CLUB/MERCADO DE LA REINA

Gran Vía 12 Ⓜ Gran Vía Ⓦ mercadodelareina .es. Gin Club 1.30pm–late, bar & tapas: Mon–Thurs & Sun 9am–midnight, Fri & Sat 9am–1am, restaurant: 1.30–4pm & 8.30pm–midnight. MAP PP.82–83, POCKET MAP G10 & F10

A tapas bar, restaurant and *bar de copas*. The bar serves a wide range of *pinchos* and *raciones* as well as a house special (upmarket) hamburger meal at €10.50. The restaurant is rather more pricey, with main courses around €15. At the back, with its mirrored ceilings and black leather chairs, is the *Gin Club* cocktail bar, offering over twenty different brands.

TABERNA ÁNGEL SIERRA

C/Gravina 11 Ⓜ Chueca. Daily noon–2am. MAP PP.82–83, POCKET MAP G3

One of the great bars in Madrid, where everyone drinks *vermút* accompanied by free, exquisite pickled anchovy tapas. *Raciones* are also available in the seated area, though they are a little pricey.

Clubs

BARCO

C/Barco 24 Ⓜ Tribunal Ⓦ barcobar.com. Mon–Thurs & Sun 10pm–5.30am, Fri & Sat 10pm–6am. MAP PP.82–83, POCKET MAP E4

Popular venue in the midst of the increasingly fashionable Triball district, *BarCo* hosts regular concerts and jam sessions, while the DJs take over late night with an eclectic selection of music – anything from the latest funk and hip hop to 80s classics.

BASH

Plaza Callao 4 Ⓜ Callao Ⓦ tripfamily.com. Wed 11pm–6am, Thurs–Sat midnight–6am, Sun midnight–5am. €12–15, including two drinks. MAP PP.82–83, POCKET MAP E4

Bash is one of the major venues on the Madrid club scene. The *OHM Dance Club* techno-house sessions on Fridays and Saturdays (plus one Sunday a month, for those with real stamina) are a mainstay of the gay scene.

TUPPERWARE

C/Corredera Alta de San Pablo 26 Ⓜ Tribunal. Daily 9pm–3.30am. MAP PP.82–83, POCKET MAP F2

A Malasaña legend with retro decor and reasonably priced drinks, this is the place to go for indie tunes, with grunge and punk era classics. Downstairs is usually packed to the rafters, but upstairs the atmosphere is more relaxed.

Salamanca and Paseo de la Castellana

Exclusive Barrio de Salamanca was developed in the second half of the nineteenth century as an upmarket residential zone under the patronage of the Marquis of Salamanca. Today, it's still home to Madrid's smartest apartments and designer emporiums, while the streets are populated by the chic clothes and sunglasses brigade, decked out in fur coats, Gucci and gold. Shopping aside, there's a scattering of sights here, including the pick of the city's smaller museums and Real Madrid's imposing Santiago Bernabéu stadium. Bordering Salamanca to the west is the multi-lane Paseo de la Castellana, peppered with corporate office blocks, where, in summer, the section north of Plaza de Colón is littered with trendy terrazas.

PLAZA DE COLÓN

Ⓜ Colón. MAP P.92. POCKET MAP H3

Overlooking a busy crossroads and dominating the square in which they stand are a Neo-Gothic monument to Christopher Columbus (Cristóbal Colón), given as a wedding gift to Alfonso XII, and an enormous Spanish flag. Directly behind are the Jardínes del Descubrimiento (Discovery Gardens), a small park containing three huge stone blocks representing Columbus's ships, the *Niña*, *Pinta* and *Santa María*. Below the plaza, underneath a cascading wall of water, is the **Teatro Fernán Gómez**, a venue

for theatre, film, dance, music and occasional exhibitions.

BIBLIOTECA NACIONAL AND MUSEO DEL LIBRO

Paseo de Recoletos 20 Ⓜ Colón Ⓦ www .bne.es. Tues–Sat 10am–8pm, Sun & hols 10am–2pm. Free. MAP P.92, POCKET MAP J3

The National Library contains over six million volumes, including every work published in Spain since 1716. The museum within displays a selection of the library's treasures, including Arab, Hebrew and Greek manuscripts, and hosts regular temporary exhibitions related to the world of art and literature.

MUSEO ARQUEOLÓGICO NACIONAL

C/Serrano 13 Ⓜ Serrano or Colón Ⓦ man.es. Tues–Sat 9.30am–8pm, Sun 9.30am–3pm. €3; Free Sat after 2pm & Sun. MAP P.92, POCKET MAP J3

Revitalised after a lengthy refurbishment, the archeological museum's collections have been given a new lease of life with their arrangement around a naturally lit central atrium, while the labelling and video explanations (in English and Spanish) put the exhibits in context. The museum holds some very impressive pieces, among them the celebrated Celto-Iberian busts known as *La Dama de Elche* and *La Dama de Baza*, and a wonderfully rich hoard of Visigothic treasures found at Toledo. The museum also contains outstanding Roman, Egyptian, Greek and Islamic finds.

MUSEO DE CERA

Paseo de Recoletos 41 Ⓜ Colón Ⓦ museo ceramadrid.com. Mon–Fri 10am–2.30pm & 4.30–8.30pm, Sat, Sun & hols 10am–8.30pm. €17 (€12 for 4–12 year olds). MAP P.92, POCKET MAP H3

Over 450 different personalities – including a host of VIPs, heads of state and, of course, Real Madrid football stars – are displayed in this expensive and tacky museum, which is nevertheless popular with children. There's also a chamber of horrors and a 3-D film history of Spain.

MUSEO DE ARTE PÚBLICO

Paseo de la Castellana 41 Ⓜ Rubén Darío. MAP P.92, POCKET MAP J1

An innovative use of the space underneath the Juan Bravo flyover, this open-air art museum is made up of a haphazard collection of sculptures, cubes, walls and fountains, including work by Eduardo Chillida, Joan Miró and Julio González.

MUSEO SOROLLA

Paseo del General Martínez Campos 37 Ⓜ Rubén Darío, Gregorio Marañon or Iglesia Ⓦ museosorolla.mcu.es. Tues–Sat 9.30am–8pm, Sun 10am–3pm. €3, free Sat 2–8pm & Sun. MAP P.92, POCKET MAP J1

Part museum and part art gallery, this tribute to an artist's life and work is one of Madrid's most underrated treasures. Situated in Joaquín Sorolla's former home, it's a delightful oasis of peace and tranquillity, its cool and shady Andalucian-style courtyard and gardens decked out with statues, fountains, assorted plants and fruit trees. The ground floor has been kept largely intact, recreating the authentic atmosphere of the artist's living and working areas. The upstairs rooms, originally the sleeping quarters, have been turned into a gallery, where sunlight, sea, intense colours, women and children dominate Sorolla's impression-istic paintings. On your way out in the Patio Andaluz, there's a collection of his sketches and gouaches.

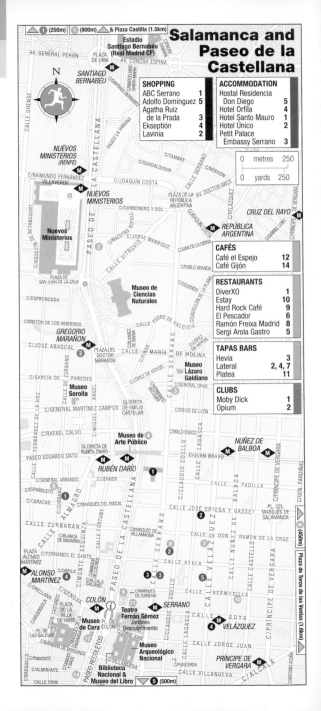

Salamanca and Paseo de la Castellana

SHOPPING
ABC Serrano	1
Adolfo Domínguez	5
Agatha Ruiz de la Prada	3
Ekseptión	4
Lavinia	2

ACCOMMODATION
Hostal Residencia Don Diego	5
Hotel Orfila	4
Hotel Santo Mauro	1
Hotel Único	2
Petit Palace Embassy Serrano	3

CAFÉS
Café el Espejo	12
Café Gijón	14

RESTAURANTS
DiverXO	1
Estay	10
Hard Rock Café	9
El Pescador	6
Ramón Freixa Madrid	8
Sergi Arola Gastro	5

TAPAS BARS
Hevia	3
Lateral	2, 4, 7
Platea	11

CLUBS
Moby Dick	1
Opium	2

MUSEO LÁZARO GALDIANO

C/Serrano 122 ⓜ Gregorio Marañón ⓦ flg
.es. Mon & Wed-Sat 10am–4.30pm, Sun
10am–3pm. €6, free 3.30–4.30pm, Sun
2–3pm. MAP P92, POCKET MAP J1

When businessman and
publisher José Lázaro Galdiano
died in 1947, he left his private
collection – a vast treasure trove
of paintings and *objets d'art* – to
the state. Spread over the four
floors of his former home, the
collection contains jewellery,
outstanding Spanish archeological pieces and some
beautifully decorated thirteenth-
century Limoges enamels.
There's also an excellent
selection of European paintings
with works by Bosch,
Rembrandt, Reynolds and
Constable, plus Spanish artists
including Zurbarán, Velázquez,
El Greco and Goya. Other
exhibits include several clocks
and watches, many of them once
owned by Emperor Charles V.

MUSEO DE CIENCIAS NATURALES

C/José Gutiérrez Abascal 2 ⓜ Gregorio
Marañón ⓦ www.mncn.csic.es. Tues-Fri, Sun
& hols 10am–5pm, Sat 10am–8pm (July &
Aug 10am–3pm). €7. MAP P92, POCKET MAP J1

The Natural History Museum's
displays are split between two
buildings. One contains a fairly
predictable collection of stuffed
animals, skeletons and audio-
visual displays on the evolution
of life on earth, the other is
home to some rather dull fossil
and geological exhibits.

ESTADIO SANTIAGO BERNABÉU

C/Concha Espina 1 ⓜ Santiago Bernabéu
☎ 902 321 809, tickets ☎ 902 324 324,
ⓦ realmadrid.com. Ticket office daily 10–7pm
(match days from 9am). Tickets from €30.
Tour and trophy exhibition: Mon-Sat
10am–7pm, Sun 10.30am–6.30pm (closes five
hours before games on match days); €19,
under-14s €13. MAP P92, POCKET MAP J1

The magnificent 80,000-seater
Bernabéu stadium provides a
suitably imposing home for one
of the most glamorous teams in
football, Real Madrid. Venue of
the 1982 World Cup final, the
stadium has witnessed countless
triumphs of "Los blancos", who
have notched up 32 Spanish
league titles and ten European
Cup triumphs in their 111-year
history. Real have broken the
world transfer record three times
in the last fifteen years, and their
latest star is Portugal forward
Cristiano Ronaldo. Tickets for
big games can be tricky to get
hold of, but the club runs a
telephone and internet booking
service (see above).

You can catch a glimpse of the
hallowed turf on the stadium
tour during which you visit the
changing rooms, walk around
the edge of the pitch and sit in
the VIP box before heading to
the trophy room with its endless
cabinets of gleaming silverware.
The tour ends with the
obligatory visit to the overpriced
club shop – where you soon
come to realize why Real is one
of the richest football clubs in
the world. The stadium also has
a reasonably priced café
(*Realcafé*) and two more
expensive restaurants (*Puerta 57*
and *Asador de la Esquina*), all
affording views over the pitch.

TROPHIES AT ESTADIO SANTIAGO BERNABÉU

PLAZA DE TOROS DE LAS VENTAS

PLAZA CASTILLA

🚇 Plaza de la Castilla. MAP P.92, POCKET MAP J1

The Paseo de la Castellana ends with a flourish at Plaza Castilla with the dramatic leaning towers of the Puerta de Europa and four giant skyscrapers constructed on Real Madrid's former training ground, the result of a controversial deal that allowed the club to solve many of its financial problems. The two tallest towers – one by Norman Foster – soar some 250 metres skywards.

PLAZA DE TOROS DE LAS VENTAS

C/Alcalá 237 🚇 Ventas ☎ 913 562 200, 🌐 las -ventas.com. Box office March–Oct Thurs–Sun 10am–2pm & 4–7pm; ☎ 902 150 025, 🌐 taqu illatoros.com. €5–150. MAP P.92, POCKET MAP K3

On the easternmost tip of the Barrio de Salamanca, Madrid's 23,000-capacity, Neo-Mudéjar bullring, Las Ventas, is the most illustrious in the world. The season lasts from March to October and *corridas* (bullfights) are held every Sunday at 7pm and every day during the three main *ferias* (fairs): La Comunidad (early May), San Isidro (mid-May to June) and Otoño (late Sept to Oct). Tickets go on sale at the ring a couple of days in advance, though many are already allocated to season-ticket holders. The cheapest seats are *gradas*, the highest rows at the back; the front rows are known as the *barreras*. Seats are also divided into *sol* (sun), *sombra* (shade) and *sol y sombra* (shaded after a while), with *sombra* the most expensive.

There's a refurbished taurine **museum** attached to the bull-ring (March–Oct Tues–Fri 9.30am–2.30pm, Sun & fight days 10am–1pm; Nov–Feb Mon–Fri 9.30am–2pm; free) with an intriguing collection of memorabilia including stunning *trajes de luces*, the beautifully decorated suits worn by the *toreros*. You can also step onto the sand yourself with a tour of the bullring (daily 10am–6pm, 10am–2pm on *corrida* days; €10 with audioguide).

Bullfighting

The bullfight is a classic image of Spain, but the ethical arguments against it are well-known – the governments of Catalunya and the Canary Islands have gone so far as to ban it. Spain's main opposition to bullfighting is organised by ADDA (🌐 addaong.org), whose website has information about international campaigns and current actions. To aficionados, the bulls are a ritual part of Spanish culture, with the emphasis on the way man and bull "perform" together. Fighting bulls are, they will tell you, bred for the industry; they live a reasonable life before they are killed, and if the bullfight went, so, too, would the bulls. If you decide to attend a *corrida*, try to see a big, prestigious event, where star performers are likely to despatch the bulls with "art" and a "clean" kill; there are few sights worse than a matador making a prolonged, messy kill.

Shops

ABC SERRANO

Paseo de la Castellana 34 and C/Serrano 61, both Ⓜ Rubén Darío Ⓦ abcserrano.com. Mon–Sat 10am–9pm, Sun noon–8pm. MAP P.92, POCKET MAP J1

Upmarket shopping mall housed in the beautiful former headquarters of the ABC newspaper. There are fashion and household outlets, as well as a couple of bars and restaurants, and a popular rooftop terrace.

ADOLFO DOMÍNGUEZ

C/Serrano 5 Ⓜ Retiro. Mon–Sat 10am–8.30pm. MAP P.92, POCKET MAP J4

Domínguez has opened a massive five-storey flagship store for his slightly sober but elegant modern Spanish designs – a wide range of natural colours and free lines for both men and women.

AGATHA RUIZ DE LA PRADA

C/Serrano 27 Ⓜ Serrano Ⓦ agatharuizdela prada.com. Mon–Sat 10am–8.30pm. MAP P.92, POCKET MAP J2

Movida-era designer who shows and sells her gaudily coloured clothes and accessories at this dazzling outlet. There's a children's line, stationery and household goods too.

EKSEPTIÓN

C/Velázquez 28 Ⓜ Velázquez Ⓦ ekseption.es. Mon–Sat 10.30am–8.30pm. MAP P.92, POCKET MAP K3

A dramatic catwalk bathed in spotlights leads into this shop selling some of the most expensive women's clothes in Madrid. Next door are younger, more casual clothes in the Eks shop for both men and women. There is also a branch selling discount last-season fashions at half-price at Avenida Concha Espina 14 (Mon–Sat 11am–7pm).

LAVINIA

C/José Ortega y Gasset 16 Ⓜ Nuñez de Balboa Ⓦ lavinia.es. Mon–Sat 10am–9pm, first Sun in month noon–8pm. MAP P.92, POCKET MAP K1

A massive wine shop with a great selection from Spain and the rest of the world. The perfect place to get that Ribera del Duero, Albariño or Rueda that you wanted to take home.

Cafés

CAFÉ EL ESPEJO

Paseo de Recoletos 31 Ⓜ Colón Ⓦ restauranteelespejo.com. Daily 9am–1am. MAP P.92, POCKET MAP H3

Opened in 1978, but you wouldn't guess it from the antiquated decor – think mirrors, gilt and a wonderful, extravagant glass pavilion. The leafy terraza is an ideal spot to enjoy a coffee and watch the world go by.

CAFÉ GIJÓN

Paseo de Recoletos 21 Ⓜ Colón. Daily 8am–1.30am. MAP P.92, POCKET MAP H4

A famous literary café dating from 1888, decked out in Cuban mahogany and mirrors. A centre of the *Movida* in the 1980s, it still hosts regular artistic *tertulias* (discussion groups). There is a restaurant, but you're best off sticking to drinks in the bar or on the pleasant summer terraza.

AGATHA RUIZ DE LA PRADA

CAFÉ EL ESPEJO

Restaurants

DIVERXO

C/Padre Damian 23 Ⓜ Cuzco ☎ 915 700 766.
Ⓦ diverxo.com. Tues–Sat 2–3.30pm &
9–11.30pm. MAP P.92, POCKET MAP J1

Madrid's only three-Michelin
star restaurant, located in the
NH Eurobuilding hotel, is run by
chef David Muñoz and has a
deserved reputation for stunning
presentation, mouth-watering
food and unpretentious service.
Prices are sky-high – taster
menus are €145 and €200 – and
the waiting list is long. You have
to book months in advance,
paying a €60 charge which is
discounted from the final bill.

ESTAY

C/Hermosilla 46 Ⓜ Velázquez ☎ 915 780 470.
Ⓦ estayrestaurante.com, Mon–Sat 1–4pm &
8pm–midnight. MAP P.92, POCKET MAP K2

Basque-style cuisine in
miniature (canapés and mini
casseroles) in this pleasant,
roomy restaurant. A great range
of *pintxos*, including *jamón* with
roquefort cheese, langoustine
vol-au-vents and a fine wine list
too. A meal will cost €25–30.

HARD ROCK CAFÉ

Paseo de la Castellana 2 Ⓜ Colón ☎ 914 364
340. Daily 12.30pm–2am. MAP P.92, POCKET MAP J2

A children's favourite, with its
tried-and-tested formula of rock
memorabilia, Tex-Mex and
burgers at under €20 a head. The
best part is the summer terraza
overlooking Plaza Colón.

EL PESCADOR

C/José Ortega y Gasset 75 Ⓜ Lista ☎ 914
021 290. Mon–Sat 12.30–4pm & 7.30pm–
midnight. Closed Aug. MAP P.92, POCKET MAP K1

One of the city's top seafood
restaurants, with specials flown
in daily from the Atlantic.
Prices are high (around €55 per
head), but you'll rarely
experience better-quality
seafood than this. If funds don't
stretch to a full meal, you can
try a *ración* in the bar instead.

RAMÓN FREIXA MADRID

C/Claudio Coello 67 Ⓜ Serrano ☎ 917 818
262. Tues–Sat 1–3.30pm & 9–11pm. Closed
Easter, Aug & Christmas. MAP P.92, POCKET MAP J2

Catalan chef Ramón Freixa's
flagship Michelin-starred
restaurant in Madrid, situated in
the luxury surroundings of the
Hotel Único (see p.129) in the
heart of Salamanca. Creative
and impeccably presented dishes
from an ever-changing menu
featuring superb game, fish and
new twists on Spanish classics.
À la carte dishes are €35–65,
while taster menus are available
from €85. Only has space for 35
diners, so book well in advance,
especially if you want a table on
the summer terrace.

SERGI AROLA GASTRO

C/Zurbano 31 Ⓜ Rubén Darío ☎ 913 102 169
Ⓦ sergiarola.es. Tues–Sat 2–3.30pm &
9–11.30pm. Closed Jan–March & July–Sept.
MAP P.92, POCKET MAP H1

Former pupil of Spanish chef
extraordinaire Ferran Adrià,
Arola launched this intimate
showcase for his innovative
cuisine with his wife Sara Fort.
The seasonal menus display an
inspired range of fresh produce;
set menus are €105–€135, and
there's a €49 weekday lunchtime
menu plus a children's option
(under-14s) for €25 at Saturday
lunch. If you go à la carte,
expect to pay €50 for mains.

Tapas bars

HEVIA

C/Serrano 118 Ⓜ Rubén Darío or Gregorio
Marañon Ⓦ heviamadrid.com. Mon–Sat
9am–1am. MAP P.92, POCKET MAP J1

Plush venue for plush clientele
feasting on pricey but excellent
tapas and canapés – the hot
Camembert is delicious, as is
the selection of smoked fish.

LATERAL

Paseo de la Castellana 42 Ⓜ Rubén Darío
Ⓦ lateral.com. Mon–Wed 9am–midnight, Thurs
& Fri 9am–1am, Sat noon–1am, Sun noon–
midnight. MAP P.92 & PP.82–83, POCKET MAP J1

A swish tapas bar serving
classic dishes such as *croquetas*
and *pimientos rellenos* (stuffed
peppers) with a modern twist.
There are other branches at
C/Velázquez 57, C/Fuencarral
43, Paseo de la Castellana 89
and Plaza Santa Ana 12.

PLATEA

C/Goya 5–7 Ⓜ Colón or Serrano Ⓦ platea
madrid.com. Mon–Wed & Sun noon–12.30am,
Thurs–Sat noon–2.30am. MAP P.92, POCKET MAP J2

A gastronome's paradise: a host
of upmarket tapas bars and food
stalls run by renowned chefs,
scattered over several floors in a
former theatre by Plaza de
Colón. Spanish, Mexican,
Peruvian and Japanese
specialities are all on offer, and
there's a patisserie, a cocktail bar
and a restaurant run by Ramón
Freixa all under the same roof.

Clubs

MOBY DICK

Avda Brasil 5 Ⓜ Cuzco or Santiago Bernabéu
Ⓦ mobydickclub. Mon–Thurs 10pm–3am, Fri
& Sat 10pm–5am. MAP P.92, POCKET MAP J1

Intimate club/music venue with
a friendly atmosphere. Plays
host to a variety of Spanish
groups and the odd international star – Roddy Frame was a
recent visitor. The music ranges
from indie to pop-rock and jazz.

OPIUM

C/José Abascal Ⓜ Gregorio Marañon Ⓦ opium
madrid.com. Wed–Sun midnight–6am. €15–20
including first drink; often free entry before
1.30am. MAP P.97, POCKET MAP J1

Electronic/house music from
resident DJs in this reopened club
(its predecessor was closed for
exceeding maximum capacity).
Popular with *pijos* – fashion-
conscious rich kids – and the
upmarket glamour crowd.

PLATEA

Plaza de España and beyond

Largely constructed in the Franco era and dominated by two early Spanish skyscrapers, the Plaza de España provides an imposing full stop to Gran Vía and a breathing space from the densely packed streets to the east. Beyond the square lies a mixture of aristocratic suburbia, university campus and parkland, distinguished by the green swathes of Parque del Oeste and Casa de Campo. Sights include the eclectic collections of the Museo Cerralbo, the fascinating Museo de América, the Ermita de San Antonio de la Florida, with its stunning Goya frescoes and, further out, the pleasant royal residence of El Pardo. Meanwhile, the spacious terrazas along Paseo del Pintor Rosales provide ample opportunity for refreshment.

PLAZA DE ESPAÑA

Ⓜ Plaza de España. MAP P.100, POCKET MAP C3

The Plaza de España was the Spanish dictator Franco's attempt to portray Spain as a dynamic, modern country. The gargantuan apartment complex of the **Edificio de España**, which heads the square, looks like it was transplanted from 1920s New York, but was in fact completed in 1953. Four years later, the 32-storey **Torre de Madrid** took over for some time as the tallest building in Spain. Together they tower over an elaborate monument to Cervantes in the middle of the square, set by an uninspiring pool. The plaza itself can be a little seedy at night, although it does play

DON QUIXOTE IN PLAZA ESPAÑA

host to occasional festivities and an interesting craft fair during the fiesta of San Isidro (on or around May 15).

MUSEO DE CERRALBO

C/Ventura Rodríguez 17 Ⓜ Plaza de España Ⓦ museocerralbo.mcu.es Tues, Wed, Fri & Sat 9.30am–3pm, plus Thurs 5–8pm, Sun & hols 10am–3pm €3, free Thurs 5–8pm, Sat after 2pm & Sun. MAP P.100, POCKET MAP B3

Reactionary politician, poet, traveller and archeologist, the seventeenth Marqués de Cerralbo endowed his elegant nineteenth-century mansion with a substantial collection of paintings, furniture and armour. Bequeathed to the state on his death, the house opened as a museum in 1962 and the cluttered nature of the exhibits is partly explained by the fact that the marqués's will stipulated that objects should be displayed exactly as he had arranged them. The highlight is a fabulous over-the-top mirrored ballroom with a Tiepolo-inspired fresco, golden stuccowork and marbled decoration.

CENTRO CULTURAL CONDE DUQUE

C/Conde Duque 9–11 Ⓜ Ventura Rodríguez Ⓦ condeduquemadrid.es. MAP P.100, POCKET MAP C2

Constructed in the early eighteenth century, this former royal guard barracks has been converted into a dynamic cultural centre, housing the city's **contemporary art** collection (Mon–Fri 9am–2.30pm) and hosting a variety of exhibitions and concerts.

PLAZA DE COMENDADORAS

Ⓜ Noviciado. MAP P.100, POCKET MAP D2

Bordered by a variety of interesting craft shops, bars and cafés, this tranquil square is named after the convent that occupies one side of it. The convent is run by nuns from the military order of Santiago and the attached church is decked out with banners celebrating the victories of the Order's knights. A large painting of their patron, St James the Moor-slayer, hangs over the high altar. The plaza itself comes alive in the summer months when the terrazas open and locals gather for a chat and a drink.

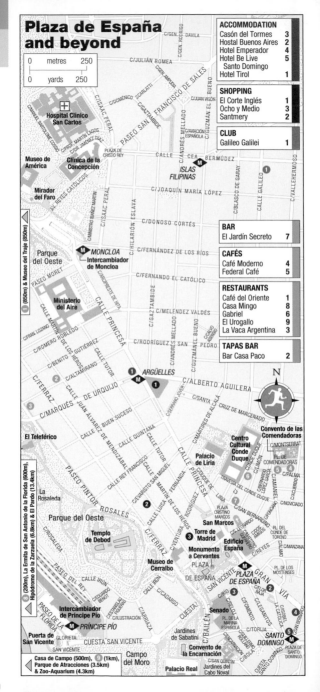

Plaza de España and beyond

ACCOMMODATION	
Casón del Tormes	3
Hostal Buenos Aires	2
Hotel Emperador	4
Hotel Be Live Santo Domingo	5
Hotel Tirol	1

SHOPPING	
El Corte Inglés	1
Ocho y Medio	3
Santmery	2

CLUB	
Galileo Galilei	1

BAR	
El Jardín Secreto	7

CAFÉS	
Café Moderno	4
Federal Café	5

RESTAURANTS	
Café del Oriente	1
Casa Mingo	8
Gabriel	6
El Urogallo	9
La Vaca Argentina	3

TAPAS BAR	
Bar Casa Paco	2

PLAZA DE COMENDADORAS

9.30am–7pm, Sun 10am–3pm. €3, free on Sun and for under-18s. MAP P.100, POCKET MAP B1

This fabulous collection of pre-Columbian American art and artefacts includes objects brought back at the time of the Spanish Conquest, as well as more recent acquisitions and donations. The layout is thematic, with sections on geography, history, social organization, religion and communication. The Aztec, Maya and Inca civilizations are well represented and exhibits include: the Madrid Codex, one of only three surviving hieroglyphic manuscripts depicting everyday Maya life; the Tudela Codex, with indigenous paintings describing the events of the Spanish Conquest; and the Quimbayas Treasure, a breathtaking collection of gold objects from a funeral treasure of the Colombian Quimbaya culture, dated 900–600 BC.

MINISTERIO DEL AIRE

Ⓜ Moncloa. MAP P.100, POCKET MAP B1

The Air Ministry is a product of the post-Civil War Francoist building boom. Work on the mammoth edifice began in 1942, and even the Third Reich's architect, Albert Speer, was consulted. However, with the defeat of the Nazis, plans were soon changed and a Habsburg-style structure was built instead – nicknamed the "Monasterio" del Aire because of its similarity to El Escorial. The neighbouring Arco de la Victoria was constructed in 1956 to commemorate the Nationalist military triumph in the Civil War.

MUSEO DE AMÉRICA

Avda de los Reyes Católicos 6 Ⓜ Moncloa Ⓦ www.mecd.gob.es/museodeamerica. Tues, Wed, Fri & Sat 9.30am–3pm, Thurs

MUSEO DE AMÉRICA

MUSEO DEL TRAJE

Avda de Juan de Herrera 2 Ⓜ Moncloa Ⓦ museodeltraje.mcu.es. Tues–Sat 9.30am–7pm, Sun & hols 10am–3pm (July & Aug open late from 9.30am–10.30pm on Thurs). €3, free Sat after 2.30pm and all day Sun. MAP P.100, POCKET MAP B1

A fascinating excursion through the history of clothes and costume. Exhibits include garments from a royal tomb dating back to the thirteenth century, some stunning eighteenth-century ballgowns and a selection of Spanish regional costumes as well as shoes, jewellery and underwear. Modern Spanish and international designers are also featured, with a Paco Rabane mini-skirt and elegant shoes from Pedro del Hierro. There is an upmarket restaurant in the grounds, which has a cool garden terrace in the summer (see p.106).

PARQUE DEL OESTE

Ⓜ Moncloa. Daily 10am–9pm. MAP P.100, POCKET MAP A2–B3

Featuring a pleasant stream, assorted statues and shady walks, this delightful park offers a welcome respite from the busy streets of the capital. In summer, there are numerous terrazas overlooking it on Paseo del Pintor Rosales. The beautiful rose garden – in C/Rosaleda – is at its most fragrant in May and June, while further down the hill is a small cemetery where the 43 Spaniards executed by occupying French troops on May 3, 1808 – and immortalized by Goya in his famous painting in the Prado (see p.66) – lie buried.

TEMPLO DE DEBOD

C/Ferraz 1 Ⓜ Plaza de España. April–Sept Tues–Fri 10am–2pm & 6–8pm, Sat & Sun 9.30am–8pm; Oct–March Tues–Fri 9.45am–1.45pm & 4.15–6.15pm, Sat & Sun 9.30am–8pm. Free. MAP P.100, POCKET MAP B3

A fourth-century BC Egyptian temple in the middle of Madrid may seem an incongruous sight. It's here, however, as a thank-you from the Egyptian government for Spanish help in salvaging archeological sites threatened by the construction of the Aswan High Dam. Reconstructed here stone by stone in 1968, it has a multimedia exhibition on the culture of Ancient Egypt inside. Archeologists have called for it to be enclosed and insulated from the open air as pollution is taking a heavy toll on the stone.

TEMPLE DE DEBOD

EL TELEFÉRICO

Paseo del Pintor Rosales Ⓜ Argüelles
Ⓦ teleferico.com. April–Sept Mon–Fri noon–
early eve (exact times vary), Sat & Sun
noon–around 8pm; Oct–March Sat, Sun &
hols noon–dusk. €4 single, €5.80 return.
MAP P.100, POCKET MAP A2

The Teleférico **cable car**
shuttles passengers from the
edge of the Parque del Oeste
high over the Manzanares river
to a restaurant/bar in the
middle of Casa de Campo (see
below). The round trip offers
some fine views of the park, the
Palacio Real, the Almudena
Cathedral and the city skyline.

LA ERMITA DE SAN ANTONIO DE LA FLORIDA

Paseo de la Florida 5 Ⓜ Príncipe Pío
Ⓦ www.munimadrid.es/ermita Tues–Sun
9.30am–8pm. Free. MAP P.100, POCKET MAP A4

Built on a Greek-cross plan
between 1792 and 1798, this
little church is the burial site of
Goya and also features some
outstanding frescoes by him.
Those in the dome depict St
Anthony of Padua resurrecting
a dead man to give evidence in
favour of a prisoner (the saint's
father) unjustly accused of
murder. The *ermita* also houses
the artist's mausoleum,
although his head was stolen by
phrenologists for examination
in the nineteenth century. The
mirror-image chapel on the
other side of the road was built
in 1925 for parish services so
that the original could become
a museum. On St Anthony's
Day (June 13), girls queue at
the church to ask the saint for a
boyfriend; if pins dropped into
the holy water then stick to
their hands, their wish will
be granted.

CASA DE CAMPO

Ⓜ Lago. MAP P.100, POCKET MAP A4

The Casa de Campo, an
enormous expanse of heath and
scrub, is in parts surprisingly
wild for a place so easily
accessible from the city.
Founded by Felipe II in the
mid-sixteenth century as a
royal hunting estate, it was only
opened to the public in 1931
and soon after acted as a base
for Franco's forces to shell the
city. Large sections have been
tamed for conventional
pastimes and there are picnic
tables and café/bars throughout
the park, the ones by the lake
providing fine views of the city.
There are also mountain-bike
trails, a jogging track, an
open-air swimming pool
(June–Sept daily 11am–8.30pm;
€5), tennis courts and rowing
boats for rent on the lake, all
near Metro Lago. The park is
best avoided after dark as many
of its roads are frequented
by prostitutes.

ZOO-AQUARIUM

Casa de Campo Ⓜ Batan Ⓦ zoomadrid.com.
Daily 10.30am–dusk. €22.95, 3–7 year olds
€18.60, under-3s free; discounts via website.
MAP P.100, POCKET MAP A4

Laid out in sections corresponding to the five continents, Madrid's zoo, on the southwestern edge of Casa de Campo, provides decent enclosures and plenty of space for over 2000 different species – though of course all of the usual animal welfare concerns about zoos apply here, too. When you've had your fill of big cats, pandas, koalas and venomous snakes, you can check out the aquarium, dolphinarium, children's zoo or bird show. Boats can be rented and there are mini train tours too.

PARQUE DE ATRACCIONES

Casa de Campo Ⓜ Batan Ⓦ parquede
atracciones.es. April–Sept most days
noon–8/9pm (midnight on Sat); Oct–March
weekends and hols noon–7pm. €31.90,
children between 90–120cm €24.90, children
under 90cm free. MAP P.100, POCKET MAP A4

This is Madrid's most popular theme park, where highlights for adults and teenagers include the 100km/hr Abismo rollercoaster, the swirling Tarantula ride, the 63-metre vertical drop La Lanzadera, the stomach-churning La Máquina and the whitewater raft ride Los Rápidos. El Viejo Caserón is a pretty terrifying haunted house, but there are some more sedate attractions too, as well as an area for younger children. Spanish acts perform in the open-air auditorium in the summer and there are frequent parades too, plus plenty of burger/pizza places to replace lost stomach contents.

HIPÓDROMO DE LA ZARZUELA

Carretera La Coruña km 8 Ⓦ hipodromodela
zarzuela.es. From €5, under-14s free. There is
a free bus that goes from Paseo de Moret next
to the Intercambiador in Moncloa. MAP P.100,
POCKET MAP A4

The horseracing track just out of the city on the A Coruña road holds races every Sunday in the spring and autumn. If you enjoy horseracing (bearing in mind the usual ethical issues involved), you'll find that the unstuffy atmosphere and beautiful setting can make this a fun day out for all the family.

EL PARDO

C/Manuel Alonso Ⓦ www.patrimonionacional
.es. Daily: April–Sept 10am–8pm; Oct–March
10am–6pm; closed for official visits. Guided
tours €9, 5–16 year-olds €4, free for EU
citizens Wed & Thurs: April–Sept 5–8pm;

MADRID ZOO

Oct–March 3–6pm. Buses (#601) from Moncloa (daily 6.30am–midnight; every 10–15min; 25min). MAP P.100, POCKET MAP A4

Nine kilometres northwest of central Madrid lies Franco's former principal residence at El Pardo. A garrison still remains at the town, where most of the Generalíssimo's staff were based, but the place is now a popular excursion for *Madrileños*, who come here for long lunches at the excellent terraza restaurants. The tourist focus is the **Palacio del Pardo**, rebuilt by the Bourbons on the site of the hunting lodge of Carlos I and still used by visiting heads of state. Behind the imposing but blandly symmetrical facade, the interior houses the chapel where Franco prayed, and the theatre where he used to censor films. On display are a number of mementos of the dictator, including his desk, a portrait of Isabel la Católica and an excellent collection of tapestries. With its highly ornate interior, the country house retreat known as the Casita del Príncipe, designed by Prado architect Juan de Villanueva for Carlos IV and his wife María Luisa de Parma, is also open for visits after a lengthy refurbishment.

Shops

EL CORTE INGLÉS

C/Princesa 41 & 56 Ⓜ Argüelles. Mon–Sat 10am–10pm, Sun 11am–9pm. MAP P.100, POCKET MAP B1

One of many branches of Spain's biggest and most popular department store. It stocks everything from souvenirs and gift items to clothes and electrical goods. Prices are on the high side, but quality is usually very good.

OCHO Y MEDIO

C/Martín de los Heros 11 Ⓜ Plaza de España. Mon 1.30–10pm, Tues–Sat 12.30–10.30pm, Sun 4–10.30pm. MAP P.100, POCKET MAP C3

Fascinating cinema bookshop with a pleasantly anarchic collection of books and film star-backed products, as well as a great terrace and small café. Perfect for a stop before watching one of the original version films in the nearby Cines Princesa.

SANTMERY

C/Juan Álvarez Mendizábal 27 Ⓜ Ventura Rodríguez Ⓦ bodegassantmery.com. Mon–Fri 9.30am–3pm & 5.30–10pm, Sat 9.30am–3pm. MAP P.100, POCKET MAP B2

Wine shop that doubles as a bar and delicatessen. You can sample some wines by the glass and try their house speciality *mousse de cabrales a la sidra* (blue cheese and cider paté).

Cafés

CAFÉ MODERNO

Plaza de las Comendadoras 1 Ⓜ Noviciado Ⓦ cafemodernomadrid.com. Daily 1pm–2.30am. MAP P.100, POCKET MAP D2

Relaxing café-bar serving good-value drinks and snacks with a busy summer terraza, situated on one of the city's nicest squares. There are two other decent café-bars alongside if this one is too crowded.

FEDERAL CAFÉ

Plaza Comendadoras 9 Ⓜ Plaza España Ⓦ federalcafe.es. Mon–Thurs 8am–midnight, Fri 8am–1am, Sat 9am–1am, Sun 9am–5.30pm. MAP P.100, POCKET MAP D2

Relaxing and spacious café with large windows looking out onto a pleasant plaza. *Federal* serves up good coffee, breakfasts and snacks, although service can be a bit hit and miss. With its free wi-fi and large tables, it's just the place to catch up on your emails, do some work or read the paper.

Restaurants

CAFÉ DEL ORIENTE

Avda. Juan de Herrera 2 Ⓜ Ciudad Universitaria Ⓣ 915 502 055. Café daily 9am–7pm, restaurant Fri 9pm–midnight, Sat 1.30–4.30pm & 9pm–1am. MAP P.100, POCKET MAP B1

Situated in the delightful pine-fringed grounds of the Museo del Traje, this Basque-influenced restaurant run by chef Delia Bautista serves two set menus at €48 and €52, with offerings such as suckling pig or seabass.

CASA MINGO

Paseo de la Florida 34 Ⓜ Príncipe Pío Ⓣ 915 477 918, Ⓦ casamingo.es. Daily 11am–midnight. Closed Aug. MAP P.100, POCKET MAP A4

Crowded and reasonably priced Asturian chicken-and-cider house. The spit-roast chicken is practically compulsory, though the chorizo cooked in cider and

CASA MINGO

cabrales (blue cheese) is also very good. Around €15 a head.

GABRIEL

C/Conde Duque 10 ⓂPlaza España ☎915 428 019, Ⓦrestaurantegabriel.com. Mon 10am–4pm, Tues–Sat 10am–2am. MAP P.100, POCKET MAP C2

Serving up an excellent home-made lunchtime menu for around €14 and some carefully selected à la carte dishes in the evenings, this is a deservedly popular restaurant on one of the most pleasant streets in this part of the city. The *croquetas de bacalao* (cod) are recommended, and to finish off they do a mean mojito.

EL UROGALLO

Lago de la Casa del Campo ⓂLago ☎915 262 369, Ⓦelurogallo.net. Tues–Sun 8.30am–midnight. MAP P.100, POCKET MAP A4

On the shores of the artificial lake in Casa de Campo, this bar-restaurant has superb views of the Palacio Real and cathedral – perfect for a lazy lunch. Eating à la carte is expensive but there's a €15 lunchtime menu.

LA VACA ARGENTINA

Paseo del Pintor Rosales 52 ⓂArgüelles ☎915 596 605, Ⓦlavacaargentina.net. Daily 1–5pm & 9pm–midnight. MAP P.100, POCKET MAP A1

One of a chain of restaurants serving Argentine-style grilled steaks (*churrasco*). This branch has good views of the Parque del Oeste from its summer terrace, but service can be slow. Average cost is around €35.

Tapas bar

BAR CASA PACO

C/Altamirano 38 ⓂArgüelles ☎915 432 821, Ⓦbarcasapaco.es. Mon–Sat 9am–11.30pm. MAP P.100, POCKET MAP A1

Old-style bar close to Parque del Oeste that's been around since the mid-fifties and serves

EL JARDÍN SECRETO

up some of the best tortillas in town, including tasty variations with prawns, goats' cheese, spinach, and steak.

Bar

EL JARDÍN SECRETO

C/Conde Duque 2 ⓂVentura Rodríguez or Plaza de España Ⓦeljardinsecretomadrid.com. Mon, Tues & Wed 5.30pm–12.30am, Thurs 6.30pm–1.30am, Fri & Sat 6.30pm–2.30am, Sun 5.30pm–12.30am. MAP P.100, POCKET MAP C2

Cosy, dimly lit bar on the corner of a tiny plaza close to Plaza de España serving reasonably priced drinks and cocktails. Service is friendly and the atmosphere unhurried.

Club

GALILEO GALILEI

C/Galileo 100 ⓂIslas Filipinas Ⓦsala galileogalilei.com. Daily 9pm–4.30am. €5–15. MAP P.100, POCKET MAP C1

Bar, concert venue and disco rolled into one. Latin music is regularly on offer, along with cabaret and flamenco.

Day-trips

If you want to take a break from the frenetic activity of the city centre, there are some fascinating day-trips all within easy reach of the Spanish capital.

If you only have time for one day-trip, make it **Toledo**. The city preceded Madrid as the Spanish capital and is today a monument to the many cultures – Visigothic, Moorish, Jewish and Christian – which have shaped the destiny of Spain. Immortalized by El Greco, who lived and worked here for most of his later career, the city is packed with memorable sights. A close second is stunning **Segovia**, with its stunning Roman aqueduct, fantasy castle and mountain backdrop. Third on the list is **El Escorial**, home to Felipe II's vast monastery-palace complex, a monument to out-monument all others, although the adjacent Valle de los Caídos, built under the orders of Franco, is even more megalomaniacal and far more chilling. And not forgetting **Aranjuez**, an oasis in the parched Castilian plain famed for its strawberries, lavish Baroque palace and gardens, and the plaza at nearby **Chinchón**, which provides a fabulous setting for a long, lazy lunch.

Day-trips

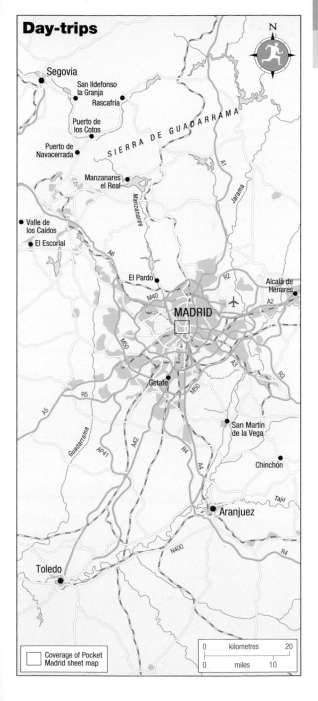

N

Segovia

San Ildefonso
la Granja

Rascafría

Puerto de
los Cotos

Puerto de
Navacerrada

SIERRA DE GUADARRAMA

A1

Jarama

Manzanares
el Real

Manzanares

Valle de
los Caídos

El Escorial

A6

El Pardo

R2

Alcalá de
Henares

A2

MADRID

M40

M50

Getafe

M50

San Martín
de la Vega

A3

R3

R5

A5

Guadarrama

AP41

A42

R4

A4

Chinchón

Taju

Aranjuez

N400

R4

Toledo

	Coverage of Pocket	0	kilometres	20
	Madrid sheet map	0	miles	10

Toledo

EL ALCÁZAR AND MUSEO DEL EJÉRCITO

C/Unión s/n Ⓦ www.museo.ejercito.es.
Thurs–Tues 11am–5pm. €5, under-18 free,
free Sun.

If one building dominates Toledo, it's the imposing fortress of the **Alcázar.** Originally the site of a Roman palace, Emperor Charles V ordered the construction of the current fortress in the sixteenth century, though it has been burned and bombarded so often that little remains of the original building. The monument enjoyed iconic status during the Franco era after the Nationalist forces inside, under siege by the Republican town, were eventually relieved by an army heading for Madrid which took severe retribution on the local inhabitants. After a tortuous relocation and refurbishment programme, the Alcázar is now home to an impressive new army museum. Encompassing a new building constructed over the archeological remains of the original fortress, the museum provides two fascinating routes – one historic and one thematic – through which the role of the Spanish military is examined in exhaustive detail. Exhibits include everything from medieval swords and suits of armour to toy soldiers and Civil War uniforms.

HOSPITAL Y MUSEO DE SANTA CRUZ

C/Cervantes 3. Mon–Sat 10am–6.30pm, Sun
10am–2pm. Free.

A superlative Renaissance building with a magnificent Plateresque main doorway, this refurbished museum houses some of the greatest El Grecos in Toledo, including *The Immaculate Conception* and *The Holy Family*. As well as outstanding works by Luca Giordano and Ribera, there's an impressive collection of exhibits dating from prehistory through to the twentieth century, including archeological finds, ceramics and sculpture.

Visiting Toledo

There are **buses** to Toledo from the bus station in Plaza Elíptica (🚇Plaza Elíptica) in Madrid every thirty minutes, taking about 1hr. The city's bus station is in the modern part of the city; bus #5 runs from it to central Plaza de Zocódover. A high-speed train service from Atocha takes just 30min; it's €20 for a day return ticket, but purchase this in advance on 🌐renfe.com. Toledo's train station is a 20min walk or a bus ride (#5 or #6) from the heart of town. The main **tourist office** (daily 10am–6pm; ☎925 254 030, 🌐www.toledo-turismo.com) is opposite the cathedral in the Plaza del Consistorio. There's another office (Mon–Fri 10am–5pm, Sat & Sun 10am–3.50pm) at the top of the escalators leading into the city from the Glorieta de La Reconquista, and one outside the city walls opposite the Puerta Nueva de Bisagra (Mon–Fri 10am–5pm, Sat & Sun 10am–7pm). You can save on the entry fees to some of the sights if you invest in the €8 Bono Turístico ticket or the Toledo Card (€18–65; 🌐toledocard.com).

LA CATEDRAL

C/Cardenal Cisneros 🌐catedralprimada.es. Mon–Sat 10am–6pm, Sun 2–6pm. Coro closed Sun am; museums closed Mon. €7, free Sun pm for Spanish citizens; audio-guides €3.

Toledo's stunning cathedral reflects the importance of the city that for so long outshone its neighbour, Madrid. A robust Gothic construction, which took over 250 years (1227–1493) to complete, it's richly decorated in Gothic, Renaissance and Baroque styles. The cavernous interior is home to some magnificent stained glass, an outstanding **Coro** (Choir), a wonderful **Gothic Capilla Mayor** (Main Chapel) and an extravagant high altar. The cathedral **museums** are worth a look for their impressive collections including paintings by El Greco, Goya and Velázquez, as well as one of El Greco's few surviving pieces of sculpture.

SANTO TOMÉ AND THE BURIAL OF THE COUNT OF ORGAZ

Plaza del Conde 🌐www.santotome.org. Daily: mid-March–mid-Oct 10am–6.45pm; mid-Oct to mid-March 10am–5.45pm. €2.50.

Housed alone, in a small annexe of the church of Santo Tomé,

one of the most celebrated attractions of Toledo is El Greco's masterpiece, *The Burial of the Count of Orgaz*. The painting depicts the count's funeral, at which St Stephen and St Augustine appeared in order to lower him into the tomb. Combining El Greco's genius for the mystic with his great powers as a portrait painter and master of colour, the work includes a depiction of the artist himself – he can be spotted seventh from the left, looking out at the viewer with his son in the foreground.

MUSEO DEL GRECO

C/Samuel Levi 🌐museodelgreco.mcu.es. April–Sept Tues–Sat 9.30am–8pm, Sun 10am–3pm; Oct–March Tues–Sat 9.30am–6.30pm, Sun 10am–3pm. €3, €5 entry with Museo Sefardí, free Sat after 2pm & Sun.

This museum in the former Jewish quarter close to Santo Tomé is devoted to the life and work of the ground-breaking sixteenth-century artist so closely associated with Toledo. A refurbished exhibition space houses his famous **View and Map of Toledo**, a series of the Twelve Apostles, completed later than the set in the cathedral, and other outstanding works.

🍴 There are plenty of bars and restaurants scattered around the old town, although inevitably most of the options are pretty touristy. For a budget option try *Casa Ludeña* at Plaza Magdalena 13, close to the Alcázar, while *Casa Aurelio* at C/Sinagoga 1 & 6, near the cathedral, offers regional specialities at reasonable prices. For a more sophisticated option try *Los Cuatro Tiempos* at C/Sixto Ramón Parro 5.

MUSEO DE VICTORIO MACHO

Plaza de Victorio Macho ⓦrealfundaciontoledo.es. Mon–Sat 10am–7pm, Sun 10am–3pm. €3.

Splendidly situated on a spur overlooking the Tajo, this museum contains the sculptures, paintings and sketches of Spanish artist Victorio Macho (1887–1966). The museum is set in a delightfully tranquil garden with the auditorium on the ground floor showing a documentary film (available in English) about the city and its history.

MUSEO SEFARDÍ/SINAGOGA DEL TRÁNSITO

C/Samuel Levi ⓦmuseosefardi.mcu.es. Tues–Sat 9.30am–6pm (summer until 7.30pm), Sun 10am–3pm. €3, free Sat after 2pm & Sun.

Built along Moorish lines by Samuel Levi in 1366, the Sinagoga del Tránsito became a church after the fifteenth-century expulsion of the Jews and was restored to its original form only in the last century. The interior is a simple galleried hall, brilliantly decorated with polychromed stuccowork and superb filigree windows, while Hebrew inscriptions praising God, King Pedro and Samuel Levi adorn the walls. It also houses a small but engaging Sephardic Museum (same hours) tracing the distinct traditions and development of Jewish culture in Spain.

SINAGOGA SANTA MARÍA LA BLANCA

C/Reyes Católicos 4. Daily: summer 10am–6.45pm; winter 10am–5.45pm. €2.50, free Wed after 4pm for EU citizens.

The second of Toledo's two surviving synagogues, the tranquil Santa María la Blanca pre-dates the Sinagoga del Tránsito by over a century. Despite having been both a church and synagogue, the horseshoe arches and the fact that it was built by Mudéjar craftsmen give it the look of a mosque. The arches are decorated with elaborate plaster designs of pine cones and palm trees, while its Baroque *retablo* (altarpiece) dates from the time it was a church. The whole effect is stunning, all set off against a deep-red floor that contains some of the original decorative tiles.

MONASTERIO DE SAN JUAN DE LOS REYES

C/San Juan de los Reyes 2. Daily: summer 10am–6.45pm; winter 10am–5.45pm. €2.50.

The exterior of this beautiful church is bizarrely festooned with the chains worn by Christian prisoners from Granada, who were released on the reconquest of the city in 1492. It was originally a **Franciscan convent** founded by the Reyes Católicos (Catholic Monarchs) Fernando and Isabel – who completed the Christian reconquest of Spain – and in which, until the fall of Granada, they had planned to be buried. Its double-storeyed cloister is outstanding, with an elaborate Mudéjar ceiling in the upper floor.

CONVENTO DE SANTO DOMINGO ANTIGUO

Plaza Santo Domingo Antiguo. Summer: Mon-Sat 11am-1.30pm & 4-7pm, Sun 4-7pm. €2.

The Convento de Santo Domingo Antiguo's chief claim to fame is as the resting place of El Greco, whose remains lie in the crypt that can be glimpsed through a peephole in the floor. The convent's religious treasures are displayed in the old choir, but more interesting is the high altarpiece of the church – El Greco's first major commission in Toledo. Unfortunately, most of the canvases have gone to museums and are here replaced by copies.

MEZQUITA DEL CRISTO DE LA LUZ

Cuesta de los Carmelitas Descalzos 10. Summer: Mon-Fri 10am-2pm & 3.30-6.40pm, Sat & Sun: 10am-6.40pm; winter: Mon-Fri 10am-2pm & 3.30-5.45pm, Sat & Sun 10am-5.45pm. €2.50.

Although this is one of the oldest Moorish monuments in Spain (the mosque was built by Musa Ibn Ali in the tenth century on the foundations of a Visigothic church), only the nave, with its nine different cupolas, is the original Arab construction. The apse was added when the building was converted into a church, and is claimed to be the first product of the Mudéjar style. The mosque itself, set in a tiny patio-like park and open on all sides to the elements, is so small that it seems more like a miniature summer pavilion, but it has an elegant simplicity of design that few of the town's great monuments can match.

LA CATEDRAL, TOLEDO

Segovia

THE AQUEDUCT

Plaza del Azoguejo.

Over 700m long and almost
30m high, Segovia's aqueduct is
an impressive sight. Built
without a drop of mortar or
cement, it has been here since
around the end of the first
century AD – no one knows
exactly when – though it no
longer carries water to the city.
For an excellent view of both
the aqueduct and the city,
climb the stairs beside it up to
a surviving fragment of the
city walls.

LA CATEDRAL

Plaza Mayor. Daily: April–Oct Mon–Sat
9.30am–7pm, Sun 1–7pm; Nov–March Mon–Sat
9.30am–6pm, Sun 1–6pm. €3. Open for mass
Sun morning; free. Museum same hours.

Segovia's cathedral was the last
major Gothic building
constructed in Spain. Pinnacles
and flying buttresses are tacked
on at every conceivable point,
although the interior is
surprisingly bare and its space is
cramped by a great green marble
choir in the very centre. The
cathedral's treasures are almost
all confined to the museum.

THE ALCÁZAR

Plaza Reina Victoria Eugenia ⓦwww
.alcazardesegovia.com. Daily: April–Sept
10am–7pm; Oct–March 10am–6pm. €5, free
for EU citizens Tues 2–4pm.

At the edge of town and
overlooking the valley of the
Eresma river is the Alcázar, an
extraordinary fantasy of a castle
with its narrow towers and
flurry of turrets. Although it
dates from the fourteenth and
fifteenth centuries, it was
almost completely destroyed by
a fire in 1862 and rebuilt as a
deliberately exaggerated version
of the original. Inside, the
rooms are decked out with
armour, weapons and
tapestries, but the major
attractions are the splendid
wooden sculptured ceilings and
the magnificent panoramas.

VERA CRUZ

Carretera Zamarramala. Tues 4–7pm,
Wed–Sun 10.30am–1.30pm & 4–7pm; closes
6pm Oct–March. Closed Nov. €2, free Tues pm.

This remarkable twelve-sided
church stands in the valley
facing the Alcázar. Built by the
Knights Templar in the early
thirteenth century on the
pattern of the Church of the
Holy Sepulchre in Jerusalem,
it once housed part of the

Visiting Segovia

Segovia is an easy day-trip from Madrid, with up to ten high-speed
trains daily (28min; €25 return) from Atocha and Chamartín stations,
plus **buses** operated by La Sepulvedana leaving from Moncloa bus
station (Metro Príncipe Pío; every 30min; 1hr 15min). The high-speed train
station is out of town – take bus #11 (every 15min) to the aqueduct.
There's a local **tourist office** in the Plaza Mayor at no. 10 (Mon–Sat
10am–2pm & 4–7/8pm, Sun 9.30am–5pm; ⓦturismocastillayleon.com).
A visitor reception centre is situated in the Plaza de Azoguejo (daily
10am–6.30pm; ⓦturismodesegovia.com) by the aqueduct and an
information point at the high-speed train station (Mon–Fri 8.15am–3.15pm,
Sat & Sun 10am–1.30pm & 4–6.30pm). A regular bus service from Segovia
to La Granja is operated by La Sepulvedana, leaving from the station at
Paseo Ezequiel González 12.

THE AQUEDUCT, SEGOVIA

supposed True Cross (hence its name). Today, you can climb the tower for a highly photogenic view of the city, while nearby is a very pleasant riverside walk along the banks of the tranquil Eresma river.

CONVENTO DE SAN ANTONIO EL REAL

C/San Antonio el Real ⓦ sanantonioelreal.es. Tues–Sat 10am–2pm & 4–7pm, Sun 10am–2pm. €2.

If you follow the line of the aqueduct away from the old city for about ten minutes, you will come to a little gem of a palace originally founded by Enrique IV in 1455 and containing an intriguing collection of Mudéjar and Hispano-Flemish art. The convent, part of which now serves as a luxury hotel, has some of the most beautiful **artesonado** (wooden sculptured) ceilings in the city and there's a wonderfully detailed fifteenth-century wooden Calvary in the main church.

LA GRANJA

ⓦ patrimonionacional.es. Palace open daily: April–Sept 10am–8pm; Oct–March 10am–6pm. €9; free Wed & Thurs: April–Sept 5–8pm; Oct–March 3–6pm. Gardens daily: 10am–dusk.

The summer palace of La Granja was built by the first Bourbon king of Spain, Felipe V, no doubt in another attempt to alleviate his homesickness for Versailles. Its chief appeal lies in its mountain setting and extravagant wooded grounds and gardens, but it's also worth casting an eye over the plush furnishings and fabulous tapestries of the palace which, though damaged by a fire in 1918, has been successfully restored.

Outside, the highlight of the eighteenth-century gardens is a series of majestic fountains. They're a fantastic spectacle, with some of the jets rising forty metres, but they usually only operate between Easter and July – at 1pm on Sundays and 5pm on Wednesdays and Saturdays – with special displays on May 30, July 25 and August 25 (€4).

Segovia is renowned for its delicious Castilian roasts; some of the best places to sample the local specialities are the *Mesón José María* at C/Cronista Lecea 11, just off the Plaza Mayor, *Mesón de Cándido* below the aqueduct at Plaza Azoguejo 5 and *Casa Duque* at nearby C/Cervantes 12.

El Escorial and Valle de los Caídos

EL ESCORIAL

Ⓦ patrimonionacional.es. Tues–Sun: April–Sept 10am–8pm; Oct–March 10am–6pm. €10; free Wed & Thurs: April–Sept 5–8pm; Oct–March 3–6pm.

El Escorial was the largest Spanish building of the Renaissance, built to celebrate a victory over the French in 1557 and divided into different sections for secular and religious use. Linking the two zones is the Biblioteca (Library), a splendid hall with vivid, multicoloured frescoes by Tibaldi, and containing some gorgeously executed Arabic manuscripts.

The enormous, cold, dark interior of the Basílica contains over forty altars, designed to allow simultaneous Masses to be held. Behind the main altar lies some of Felipe II's mammoth collection of saintly relics, including six whole bodies, over sixty heads and hundreds of bone fragments set in fabulously expensive caskets.

Many of the monastery's religious treasures are contained in the Sacristía and Salas Capitulares and include paintings by Titian, Velázquez and José Ribera. Below these rooms is the Panteón Real, where past Spanish monarchs lie in their gilded marble tombs. The royal children are laid in the Panteón de los Infantes and there's also a babies' tomb with room for sixty infants.

What remains of El Escorial's art collection – works by Bosch, Dürer, Titian, Zurbarán, among others that escaped transfer to the Prado – is kept in the elegant Museos Nuevos. Don't miss the Sala de Batallas, a long gallery lined with an epic series of paintings

depicting important imperial battles. Finally, there are the treasure-crammed Salones Reales (Royal Apartments), containing the austere quarters of Felipe II, with the chair that supported his gouty leg and the deathbed from which he was able to contemplate the high altar of the Basílica.

LA SILLA DE FELIPE

Around 3km out of town is the Silla de Felipe – "Felipe's Seat" – a chair carved into a rocky outcrop with a great view of the palace, and from where the king is supposed to have watched the building's construction. You can reach it on foot by following the path which starts by the arches beyond the main entrance to the Biblioteca; keep to the left as you go down the hill and then cross the main road and follow the signs. If you have a car, take the M-505 Ávila road and turn off at the sign after about 3km.

VALLE DE LOS CAÍDOS

Tues–Sun: April–Sept 10am–7pm; Oct–March 10am–6pm. €9; free Wed & Thurs 4–7pm (3–6pm Oct–March) for EU citizens.

Almost at first glance, this basilica complex, constructed by Franco after his Civil War victory, belies its claim to be a memorial to the dead of both sides. The grim, pompous

🍴 Good restaurants in El Escorial include *La Fonda Genara* at Plaza de San Lorenzo 2 (Mon–Sat 1–4pm & 9–11pm, Sun 1–4pm; ☎918 901 636), a relaxed place filled with theatrical mementos and offering a wide range of delicious Castilian cuisine. Set menus available for around €16, otherwise around €30 per person.

architectural forms employed, the constant inscriptions "Fallen for God and for Spain" and the proximity to El Escorial clue you in to its true function – the glorification of General Franco and his regime. The dictator himself lies buried behind the high altar, while the only other named tomb is that of his guru, the Falangist leader, José Antonio Primo de Rivera. The "other side" is present only in the fact that the whole thing was built by the Republican army's survivors.

Above the basilica is a vast 150m-high cross, reputedly the largest in the world and visible for miles around. The socialist government of José Luis Rodríguez Zapatero tried to depoliticize the site, and it was mooted that Franco's remains might be removed from the basilica, but this was rejected when the new right of-centre Popular Party returned to power in the 2011 general election.

Visiting El Escorial

There are around 25 **trains** a day to El Escorial from Madrid (5.45am–11.30pm from Atocha, calling at Chamartín), or **buses** (#661 and #664 from the intercambiador at Moncloa) run every fifteen minutes on weekdays and hourly at weekends. To visit the Valle de los Caídos from El Escorial, take a local bus run by Herranz (#660), which starts from the bus station at C/Juan de Toledo 3, just north of the visitor's entrance to the monastery. It departs at 3.15pm and returns at 5.30pm, giving you more than enough time to look around the complex.

Aranjuez and Chinchón

THE PALACIO REAL

🌐 patrimonionacional.es. Tues–Sun: April–Sept 10am–8pm; Oct–March 10am–6pm. €9; free for EU citizens Wed & Thurs: April–Sept 5–8pm; Oct–March 3–6pm.

The centrepiece of Aranjuez is the Palacio Real and its gardens. The present building dates from the 1700s and was an attempt by Spain's Bourbon monarchs to create a Spanish Versailles. The palace is noted for its exotic decor highlighted in the fabulously elaborate Porcelain and Smoking Rooms.

JARDÍN DE LA ISLA AND JARDÍN DEL PRÍNCIPE

Daily: 8am–dusk. Free.

Two palace gardens worthy of a visit are the Jardín de la Isla with its fountains and neatly tended gardens, and the more attractive Jardín del Príncipe, which inspired Rodrigo's famous *Concierto de Aranjuez*, offering

El Rana Verde close to the palace and on the banks of the river at Plaza Santiago Rusiñol is probably Aranjuez's best-known restaurant and serves a selection of set menus from €17.

shaded walks along the river and plenty of spots for a siesta.

CASA DEL LABRADOR

Jardín del Príncipe. Daily: April–Sept 10am–8pm; Oct–March 10am–6pm; €5; free for EU citizens Wed & Thurs: April–Sept 5–8pm; Oct–March 3–5pm.

At the far end of the Jardín del Príncipe is the Casa del Labrador (Peasant's House), which is anything but what its name implies. The house contains more silk, marble, crystal and gold than would seem possible to cram into so small a place, as well as a huge collection of fancy clocks. Although the hotchpotch of styles will offend purists, this miniature palace still provides a fascinating insight into the tastes of the Bourbon dynasty.

THE SMOKING ROOM AT PALACIO REAL, ARANJUEZ

Visiting Aranjuez and Chinchón

From the end of April to July and September to mid-October, a weekend service on an old wooden steam train, the **Tren de la Fresa**, runs between Madrid and Aranjuez. It leaves the Museo del Ferrocarril at 10am and departs from Aranjuez at 7pm (information ☎ 902 228 822). The €30 fare (under-10s €14.90) includes a guided bus tour in Aranjuez, entry to the monuments and *fresas con nata* on the train. Standard trains leave every 15–30min from Atocha, with the last train returning from Aranjuez at about 11.30pm. **Buses** run every half-hour during the week and every hour at weekends from Estación Sur. You'll find a helpful **tourist office** in the Casa de Infantes (daily 10am–6pm; ☎ 918 910 427, ⊛ aranjuez.es).There are hourly buses (#337) from Madrid **to Chinchón** from the bus station at Avda Mediterraneo 49 near the Plaza Conde Casal, or you can reach the town from Aranjuez on the service from Avenida de las Infantas (Mon–Fri hourly, Sat & Sun 8 daily; #430). There's a small **tourist office** in the Plaza Mayor (July–Sept Mon–Fri 10am–3pm & 5–8pm, Sat & Sun 10am–3pm; Oct–June daily 10am–7pm ☎ 918 935 323, ⊛ ciudad-chinchon.com).

CASA DE LOS MARINOS (FALÚAS REALES)

Daily: April–Sept 10am–8pm; Oct–March 10am–6pm. Included with entrance to Palacio Real. April–Sept 5–8pm; Oct–March 3–5pm.

The small Casa de los Marinos museum contains the brightly coloured launches in which royalty would take to the river – try the modern equivalent with a 45-minute boat trip through the royal parks from the jetty by the bridge next to the palace (Sat & Sun 11am & 6.30pm; times may vary in summer months).

PLAZA DE TOROS

Guided tours: Mon 11.15am, 12.15pm, 1.15pm, Sat & Sun 11.15am, 12.15pm, 1.15pm, 4.15pm; €5.

Aranjuez's beautiful eighteenth-century Plaza de Toros houses an exhibition space, part of which is made up of a **bullfighting museum**, while the rest traces the town's history and royal heritage. Nearby, on C/Naranja and C/Rosa, there are a number of *corrales*, traditional-style wooden-balconied tenement blocks.

CHINCHÓN

A stroll around the elegant little town of Chinchón, followed by lunch at one of its restaurants, is a popular pastime for *Madrileños*. Noteworthy monuments include a fifteenth-century castle (not open to visitors), a picture-postcard medieval Plaza Mayor and the Iglesia de la Asunción, with a panel by Goya of *The Assumption of the Virgin*, but it is as the home of *anís* that the town is best known. To sample the local aniseed spirit, try one of the local bars or the Alcoholera de Chinchón, a shop on the Plaza Mayor – most visitors come for a tasting before eating at one of the town's traditional *mesones* (see box below).

🍴 For a classic Castillian lunch in Chinchón, try the *Mesón el Comendador, La Casa del Pregonero* or *La Balconada* overlooking the main plaza or the nearby *Mesón Cuevas del Vino*.

Accommodation

Madrid has a plentiful supply of accommodation and most of it is very central. With increasing competition in the sector, many hotels have been busy upgrading facilities in recent years and there is now a much wider range of stylish, medium-priced hotels, including the design-conscious Petit Palace and Room Mate chains. The city has a sprinkling of exclusive top-range hotels too, while if you're after a budget place to stay, go for one of the *hostales* – small, frequently family-run establishments housed in large, centrally located apartment blocks.

The main factor to consider in choosing a place is location. To be at the heart of the old town, choose the areas around Puerta del Sol, Plaza de Santa Ana or Plaza Mayor; for nightlife, Malasaña or Chueca will appeal; if you are looking for a quieter location and a bit more luxury, consider the Paseo del Prado, Recoletos or Salamanca areas; and if you are with children the areas by the main parks are good options. Another thing to bear in mind is noise. Madrid is a high-decibel city so avoid rooms on lower floors or choose a place away from the action. As for facilities, air conditioning is usual and a welcome extra in summer.

Prices given in our reviews are for the average cost of a double room.

Booking accommodation

Madrid's increasing popularity as a weekend-break destination means that it's best to book accommodation in advance if possible. Phoning or emailing is recommended; most places will understand English. It's also advisable to reconfirm the booking a few days in advance.

Hotels in the more expensive categories run special weekend offers, so it's always worth checking their websites for details. Good deals are also often available in the summer months, but it is best to avoid Spanish national holidays, when prices peak.

If you do arrive without a reservation, the tourist information service at the airport, train and bus stations can usually help (branches and contact details are under Tourist Information in the Directory section; see p.138).

Madrid de los Austrias

BED & BREAKFAST ABRACADABRA
> C/Bailén 39, 1° Ⓜ Ópera or La Latina ☎ 656 859 784, Ⓦ abracadabrabandb .com. MAP PP.30–31, POCKET MAP C7. A homely seven-bedroom B&B run by a very friendly couple who have refurbished the place in rustic, colonial style. Some rooms have en-suite bathrooms. Continental breakfast included in the rate. Doubles with shared bathroom from €54. **En-suite doubles from €71.**

HOSTAL LA MACARENA
> C/Cava de San Miguel 8, 2° Ⓜ Sol ☎ 913 659 221, Ⓦ www.silserranos.com. MAP PP.30–31, POCKET MAP B13. Family-run *hostal* in a back street just beside Plaza Mayor. The neat, well-kept rooms are on the small side, but all have bathroom, satellite TV and a/c. It can be a little noisy, but the location is perfect. **Doubles from €64.**

HOSTAL MADRID
> C/Esparteros 6 Ⓜ Sol ☎ 915 220 060, Ⓦ hostal-madrid.info. MAP PP.30–31, POCKET MAP D12. In a fantastic setting between Sol and Plaza Mayor, this no frills *hostal* is renowned for its clean, en-suite, a/c rooms and friendly service. Rooms are small and can be a little noisy, but this is more than compensated for by the location. **Doubles from €78.**

HOSTAL TIJCAL
> C/Zaragoza 6, 3° Ⓜ Sol ☎ 913 655 910, Ⓦ hostaltijcal .com. MAP PP.30–31, POCKET MAP C12. Quirky *hostal* offering rooms (some have good views) in pastel shades with bathroom, TV, very comfortable beds and a/c. Triples and quadruples also available. A sister *hostal*, *Tijcal II*, is at C/Cruz 26 (☎ 913 604 628). **Doubles from €54.**

HOTEL MAYERLING
> C/Conde de Romanones 6 Ⓜ Tirso de Molina ☎ 914 201 580, Ⓦ mayerlinghotel .com. MAP PP.30–31, POCKET MAP D13. A stylish hotel with 22 rooms, housed in a former textile warehouse close to C/Atocha. Clean lines and black and white decor predominate in the simple, neat rooms. There's free internet and wi-fi as well as a sun terrace. **Doubles from €80.**

PETIT PALACE POSADA DEL PEINE
> C/Postas 17 Ⓜ Sol ☎ 915 238 151, Ⓦ petitpalace.com. MAP PP.30–31, POCKET MAP C12. This upmarket branch of the *Petit Palace* hotel chain is situated in a refurbished building right next to the Plaza Mayor and was once the site of a seventeenth-century inn. Sleek rooms with minimalist decor and stylish fittings. Buffet breakfast. **Doubles from €95.**

POSADA DEL LEÓN DE ORO
> C/Cava Baja 12 Ⓜ La Latina ☎ 911 191 494, Ⓦ posadadelleonedoro .com. MAP PP.30–31, POCKET MAP B14. This former inn has been converted into a chic, designer hotel with seventeen large, individually decorated rooms complete with walk-in showers, flat-screen TVs and free wi-fi. Three-night minimum stay at some times of year. **Doubles from €120.**

Ópera

LOS AMIGOS HOSTEL
> C/Arenal 26, 4° Ⓜ Ópera ☎ 915 592 472, Ⓦ losamigoshostel.com. MAP P.40, POCKET MAP B11. Great backpacking option just a few minutes from Sol. Dormitories (€19 per bed) cater for four to six people, and there are a couple of communal rooms, plus free wi-fi. The staff speak English, and bed linen and use of kitchen are included. **Doubles with bathroom from €54.**

HOSTAL DON ALFONSO
> Plaza Celenque 1, 2° Ⓜ Sol ☎ 915 319 840, Ⓦ hostaldonalfonso.es. MAP P.40, POCKET MAP C11. Just off the pedestrianized shopping street C/Arenal and a stone's throw from Sol, this clean, simply furnished *hostal* has fourteen doubles, two triples and some singles, all with bathrooms, a/c and TV. **Doubles from €50.**

HOSTAL GALA
> C/Costanilla de los Ángeles 15 Ⓜ Callao ☎ 915 419 692, Ⓦ hostalgala.com. MAP P.40, POCKET MAP B10. An upmarket, very tasteful *hostal* close to the shopping areas of C/Preciados and Gran Vía. The 22 rooms have a/c, power showers and small balconies. **Doubles from €70.**

HOSTAL ORIENTE > C/Arenal 23 Ⓜ Ópera ☎ 915 480 314, Ⓦ hostaloriente.es. MAP P.40, POCKET MAP B11. Well-appointed *hostal* close to the Opera house. The nineteen classically decorated rooms are comfortable and have newly equipped bathrooms. **Doubles from €60.**

HOSTAL CENTRAL PALACE > Plaza de Oriente 2, 3º Ⓜ Ópera ☎ 915 482 018, Ⓦ centralpalacemadrid.com. MAP P.40, POCKET MAP A11. Refurbished and very friendly *hostal* with a fabulous location on the plaza. All of the airy rooms are en-suite with good facilities, a/c and flat-screen TVs, and some have views over the plaza towards the Palacio Real. Price includes breakfast. **Doubles from €90.**

HOTEL CARLOS V > C/Maestro Vitoria 5 Ⓜ Callao ☎ 915 314 100, Ⓦ bestwestern.es/hotel-carlosv. MAP P.40, POCKET MAP D11. Traditional hotel behind the Descalzas Reales monastery. Some of the a/c rooms on the fifth floor have balconies (at extra cost), though there isn't much of a view. There's an elegant lounge and café, and the hotel has a deal with a nearby car park allowing guests to use it at reduced rates. **Doubles from €90.**

HOTEL MENINAS > C/Campomanes 7 Ⓜ Ópera ☎ 915 412 805, Ⓦ hotelmeninas.com. MAP P.40, POCKET MAP B10. A stylish 37-room hotel in a quiet street near the Teatro Real. Professional staff, fantastic attic rooms and flat-screen TVs. Guests can use the gym and sauna at the nearby *Hotel Ópera* (see below). Breakfast included for web reservations. Prices vary according to availability but usually **doubles from €85.**

HOTEL ÓPERA > C/Cuesta de Santo Domingo 2 Ⓜ Ópera ☎ 915 412 800, Ⓦ hotelopera.com. MAP P.40, POCKET MAP B10. In a pleasant location near the Plaza de Oriente, this slick hotel has 79 smart rooms (some with terraces) at reasonable rates. In keeping with the name, the waiters in the restaurant entertain diners with arias from operas and *zarzuelas*. **Doubles from €85.**

HOTEL PALACIO DE SAN MARTÍN > Plaza de San Martín 5 Ⓜ Ópera ☎ 917 015 000, Ⓦ hotelpalaciosanmartin.es. MAP P.40, POCKET MAP C10. Situated in an attractive square by the Descalzas Reales monastery, this elegant hotel offers 94 spacious rooms, a small gym and sauna, plus a fine rooftop restaurant. **Doubles from €100.**

PETIT PALACE ARENAL > C/Arenal 16 Ⓜ Sol ☎ 915 644 355, Ⓦ petitpalace.com. MAP P.40, POCKET MAP C11. A member of a popular hotel chain with 64 sleek, modern rooms. All have a/c and there are special family rooms too. Another member of the chain, the *Puerta del Sol*, is close by at C/Arenal 4. **Doubles from €75.**

ROOM MATE MARIO > C/Campomanes 4 Ⓜ Ópera ☎ 915 488 548, Ⓦ room-matehotels.com. MAP P.40, POCKET MAP B10. Hip designer hotel close to the Teatro Real. Staff are friendly and the ultra-cool rooms, though compact, are well equipped with neat bathrooms, flat-screen TVs and DVD. Buffet breakfast included in price. There is a similarly trendy member of the chain, the *Laura*, at Travesía de Trujillos 3 (☎ 917 011 670) in the plaza by the Descalzas monastery. **Doubles from €65.**

Rastro, Lavapíes and Embajadores

CAT'S HOSTEL > C/Canizares 6 Ⓜ Antón Martín ☎ 913 692 807, Ⓦ catshostel.com. MAP PP.48–49, POCKET MAP E14. Certainly not your run-of-the-mill hostel, *Cat's* has an Andalusian patio and subterranean bar. Doubles are available on request, otherwise accommodation is in clean, a/c four- to twelve-bed dorms. Price includes breakfast. **Dorm bed from €12.**

HOSTAL BARRERA > C/Atocha 96, 2° Ⓜ Antón Martín ☎ 915 275 381, Ⓦ hostalbarrera.com. MAP PP.48–49, POCKET MAP G7. Upmarket fourteen-room *hostal* a short distance from Atocha station and with an English-speaking owner. The smart a/c rooms are a cut above most found in this category and the bathrooms are modern. One of the best in this part of town. Doubles from €68.

HOTEL ARTRIP > C/Valencia 11 Ⓜ Lavapiés ☎ 915 393 282, Ⓦ artriphotel.com. MAP PP.48–49, POCKET MAP F9. A new arrival on the scene, this self-styled "Art Hotel" is conveniently located close to the Reina Sofia and other art galleries. It has seventeen sleek, design-conscious rooms that combine the modern with the traditional. Buffet breakfast €5 extra. Doubles from €120.

TRYP ATOCHA > C/Atocha 83 Ⓜ Antón Martín ☎ 913 300 500, Ⓦ tryphotels.com. MAP PP.48–49, POCKET MAP G14. This large, business-style hotel, which is not far from Huertas, has 150 modern rooms with all the facilities you'd expect. Family rooms with bunks for children start at €160. Doubles from €85.

Sol, Santa Ana and Huertas

CATALONIA PLAZA MAYOR > C/Atocha 35 Ⓜ Antón Martín ☎ 913 694 409, Ⓦ hoteles-catalonia.com. MAP P.54, POCKET MAP E13 Close to Plaza Santa Ana and the Huertas area, this new business-style hotel has spacious, functional rooms with slick modern decor and comfortable beds. There's a small fitness area and jacuzzi as well as free wi-fi. Doubles from €95.

HOSTAL ALASKA > C/Espoz y Mina 7, 4° dcha Ⓜ Sol ☎ 915 211 845, Ⓦ hostalalaska.es. MAP P.54, POCKET MAP E12. Doubles, triples and a single in this friendly hostal. All seven of the basic, brightly decorated rooms have bathrooms, a/c and TV. There's an apartment available on the fifth floor with a bedroom, sofa-bed and kitchen (from €150 for six). Doubles from €55.

HOSTAL ARMESTO > C/San Agustín 6, 1° dcha Ⓜ Antón Martín ☎ 914 299 031, Ⓦ hostalarmesto.com. MAP P.54, POCKET MAP G13. Eight-room hostal with some nicely decorated rooms, all with

Our picks

Friendly – *Hostal Gonzalo* p.126
Good value – *Hostal Gala* p.123
Boutique – *Hotel Abalú* p.128
Designer chic – *Hotel Urban* p.126
Location – *Hostal Central Palace* p.124
Exclusive – *Hotel Orfila* p.128
Family – *Hotel Tirol* p.129

small bathrooms, a/c and TV. The best ones overlook the delightful little garden in the Casa de Lope de Vega next door. Very well positioned for the Huertas/Santa Ana area. Doubles from €40.

HOSTAL PERSAL > Plaza del Angel 12 Ⓜ Sol ☎ 913 694 643, Ⓦ hostalpersal.com. MAP P.54, POCKET MAP E13. Eighty-room hostal that's closer to a hotel in terms of services and facilities. The simple, clean rooms will have a/c, bathrooms, TV and free wi-fi. Triples and quadruples available from €70 and €100 respectively. Doubles from €60.

HOSTAL PLAZA D'ORT > Plaza del Angel 13, 1° Ⓜ Sol ☎ 914 299 041, Ⓦ plazadort.com. MAP P.54, POCKET MAP E13. All the smallish rooms in this very clean hostal have a shower or bath, TV, telephone and internet connection, and some have a/c too. Doubles from €40.

HOSTAL RIESCO > C/Correo 2, 3° Ⓜ Sol ☎ 915 222 692, Ⓦ hostalriesco.es. MAP P.54, POCKET MAP D12. Neat and simple rooms in this friendly family-run hostal located in a street just off Sol. All rooms (some of which are triples) are en suite and have a/c. Doubles from €58.

HOTEL SANTA ANA COLORS > C/Huertas 14, 2° izda Ⓜ Antón Martín ☎ 914 296 935, Ⓦ santaanacolors.com. MAP P.54, POCKET MAP F13. Smart hostal in the heart of Huertas with simple but modern en-suite rooms, all complete with a/c and plasma TVs. There is a self-service breakfast and a common room where you can read the paper. Doubles from €50.

HOTEL URBAN > Carrera San Jeronimo 34 ⓜ Sevilla ☎ 917 877 770, ⓦ derbyhotels.com. MAP P.54, POCKET MAP G12. Über cool, fashion-conscious, five-star hotel in the heart of town. There are 96 designer rooms with all mod cons, a rooftop pool, a summer terrace and two "pijo" cocktail bars. It even has its own small museum consisting of items from owner Jordi Clos's collection of Egyptian and Chinese art. Look out for special deals on the website. **Doubles from €175.**

HOTEL VINCCI SOHO > C/Prado 18 ⓜ Antón Martín ☎ 911 414 100, ⓦ vinccihoteles.com. MAP P.54, POCKET MAP G13. A great location in the heart of Huertas for this new, four-star 170-room hotel. Smart wooden decor and furnishings and modern facilities, though bathrooms are rather small. Worth it only if you can get one of the cheaper offers on the website. **Doubles from €120.**

ME MADRID REINA VICTORIA > Plaza de Santa Ana 14 ⓜ Sol ☎ 917 016 000, ⓦ memadrid.com. MAP P.54, POCKET MAP E13. Once a favourite haunt of bullfighters, this giant white wedding cake of a hotel that dominates the plaza is now part of the exclusive ME chain. It comes complete with the de rigueur minimalist decor, designer furnishings, high-tech fittings, a super cool penthouse bar and a chic restaurant serving fusion-style food. **Doubles from €155.**

PETIT PALACE LONDRES > C/Galdo 2 ⓜ Sol ☎ 915 314 105, ⓦ petitpalace .com. MAP P.54, POCKET MAP D11. One of a chain of the smart Petit Palace hotels that offer very good rates and services. This one is in a refurbished mansion close to Sol and has the trademark smart, well-appointed rooms with a range of facilities. **Doubles from €70.**

ROOM MATE ALICIA > C/Prado 2 ⓜ Sol ☎ 913 896 095, ⓦ room-matehotels.com. MAP P.54, POCKET MAP F13. Perched on the corner of Plaza Santa Ana, the 34-room Alicia is in a great location, if a little noisy. Seriously cool decor by interior designer Pascua Ortega, stylish rooms and unbeatable value. There are suites from €145 with great views over the plaza and if you really want to push the boat out there is a two-floored duplex at around €275. **Doubles from €90.**

Paseo del Arte and Retiro

HOSTAL GONZALO > C/Cervantes 34, 3° ⓜ Antón Martín ☎ 914 292 714, ⓦ hostalgonzalo.com. MAP PP.68–69, POCKET MAP H13. One of the most welcoming hostales in the city, tucked away close to Paseo del Prado. Fifteen bright, en-suite rooms, all of which have a/c, TV and recently refurbished bathrooms as well as free wi-fi. It's a very good-value, smart place run by charming owner Antonio and his brother Javier. **Doubles from €50.**

HOTEL LOPE DE VEGA > C/Lope de Vega 49 ⓜ Atocha ☎ 913 600 011, ⓦ hotellopedevega.com. MAP PP.68–69, POCKET MAP H13. With a great location close to the main art galleries, this hotel is a good mid-priced option. Each of the seven floors is dedicated to a theme relating to playwright Lope de Vega, while the business-style rooms are neat and comfortable. **Doubles from €85.**

HOTEL MORA > Paseo del Prado 32 ⓜ Atocha ☎ 914 201 569, ⓦ hotelmora.com. MAP PP.68–69, POCKET MAP H7. A slightly dated 62-room hotel perfectly positioned for the galleries on the Paseo del Prado. All of the refurbished rooms have a/c and some have pleasant views across the street (double glazing blocks out the worst of the traffic noise). **Doubles from €86.**

HOTEL PALACE > Plaza de las Cortes 7 ⓜ Sol ☎ 913 608 000, ⓦ westinpalacemadrid.com. MAP PP.68–69, POCKET MAP H12–13. Colossal, sumptuous hotel with every imaginable facility but none of the snootiness you might expect from its aristocratic appearance. A spectacular, glass-covered central patio and luxurious rooms are part of its charm. **Doubles from €220.**

HOTEL VILLA REAL > Plaza de las Cortes 10 Ⓜ Sol ☎ 914 203 767, Ⓦ derbyhotels.es. MAP PP.68–69, POCKET MAP G12. Aristocratic and highly original, the *Villa Real* comes complete with its own art collection owned by Catalan entrepreneur Jordi Clos. Each of the 96 elegant double rooms has a spacious sitting area (there are several suites too) and many have a balcony overlooking the plaza. The rooftop restaurant, which has some Andy Warhol originals on the wall, affords splendid views down towards the Paseo del Prado. Discount rates start at around €170, although **doubles normally start from €200.**

HOTEL VINCCI SOMA > C/Goya 79 Ⓜ Goya ☎ 914 357 545, Ⓦ vinccihoteles.com. MAP PP.68–69, POCKET MAP K3. This modern hotel, which is close to the Salamanca shops and Plaza Colón, has a sophisticated feel to it with its tasteful rooms and good service. Internet offers can bring the price down to around €100. **Doubles from €120.**

NH PASEO DEL PRADO > Plaza Cánovas del Castillo 4 Ⓜ Banco de España ☎ 914 292 887, Ⓦ nh-hotels. com. MAP PP.68–69, POCKET MAP H13. A new addition to the hotels in the area, this large, plush member of the *NH Collection* chain is attractively situated in front of the Neptune fountain on the Paseo del Prado. It's not that pricey either, given the excellent facilities and luxurious surroundings. The hotel's restaurant serves some high-class tapas too. There is a slightly cheaper sister hotel, the *NH Nacional*, just up the road at Paseo del Prado 48. **Doubles from €110.**

NH PUERTA DE ALCALÁ > C/Alcalá 66 Ⓜ Príncipe de Vergara ☎ 914 351 060, Ⓦ nh-hotels.com. MAP PP.68–69, POCKET MAP K4. Large, elegant hotel belonging to the efficient NH chain, just to the north of the Retiro, with smart rooms, professional staff, laundry facilities and a car park. Expensive, but good deals available during the summer and at weekends. Special weekend offers can bring the price down to €90. **Doubles from €120.**

LA PEPA CHIC B&B > Plaza de los Cortes 4, 7º dcha Ⓜ Banco de España ☎ 648 474 742, Ⓦ lapepa-bnb.com. MAP PP.68–69, POCKET MAP H12. Boutique accommodation in this neat B&B in the heart of the art museum quarter. The fourteen rooms have a brilliant white and red colour scheme, clean lines and functional furnishings. **Doubles from €65.**

RADISSON BLU, MADRID PRADO > C/Moratín 52, Plaza de Platería Martínez Ⓜ Atocha ☎ 915 242 626, Ⓦ radissonblu.com/pradohotel-madrid. MAP PP.68–69, POCKET MAP J14. Designer hotel located along the Paseo del Prado featuring sleek rooms in black, brown and white, photos of the Madrid skyline adorning the walls, black slate bathrooms and coffee machines. There is a spa and indoor pool, a whisky bar and a restaurant too. **Doubles from €120.**

URBAN SEA ATOCHA 113 > C/Atocha 113, 3º Ⓜ Atocha ☎ 913 692 895, Ⓦ blueseahotels.com. MAP PP.68–69, POCKET MAP G7. Just across the roundabout from Atocha station, this member of the *Blue Sea* chain contains 36 sleek but simple rooms at a very competitive price. A sun terrace on the sixth floor and the location make this a good option. **Doubles from €80.**

Gran Vía, Chueca and Malasaña

HOSTAL SIL/SERRANOS > C/Fuencarral 95, 2º & 3º Ⓜ Tribunal ☎ 914 488 972, Ⓦ silserranos.com. MAP PP.82–83, POCKET MAP F2. Two friendly *hostales* located at the quieter end of C/Fuencarral in Malasaña. A variety of simple but comfortable rooms all with a/c, modern bathrooms and TV. Triples and quadruples available. **Doubles from €64.**

HOSTAL ZAMORA > Plaza Vázquez de Mella 1, 4º izqda Ⓜ Gran Vía ☎ 915 217 031, Ⓦ hostalzamora.com. MAP PP.82–83, POCKET MAP F4. Seventeen simple rooms in an agreeable family-run place, most of which overlook the plaza.

All rooms have a/c, modern bathrooms and TV. There are good-value family rooms too. **Doubles from €50.**

HOTEL ABALÚ > C/Pez 19, 1°
Ⓜ Noviciado ☎ 915 314 744,
Ⓦ hotelabalu.com. MAP PP.82–83, POCKET MAP E3. This boutique hotel, which is just north of Gran Vía, has vibrant Luis Delgado-designed rooms, each one brimming with individual touches such as mini-chandeliers, butterfly prints and patterned mirrors. Personal service guaranteed. **Doubles from €75.**

HOTEL AROSA > C/Salud 21 Ⓜ Gran Vía ☎ 915 321 600, Ⓦ hotelarosa.es. MAP PP.82–83, POCKET MAP E10. Right in the heart of town, the *Arosa* has 126 spacious, a/c rooms. The standard rooms are functional, but there are sixteen more expensive oriental-style "zen" rooms with extras such as a plasma TV, free mini-bar, bathrobe and slippers. Some of the surrounding streets are a little down-at-heel, but don't let this put you off. **Doubles from €80.**

HOTEL DE LAS LETRAS > Gran Vía 11 Ⓜ Gran Vía ☎ 915 237 980, Ⓦ hoteldelasletras.com. MAP PP.82–83, POCKET MAP F10. An elegant design-conscious hotel housed in a lovely early nineteenth-century building at the smarter end of Gran Vía. The stylish, high-ceilinged rooms decorated with literary quotations come complete with plasma TVs. Downstairs, there's a smooth bar and lounge area and a high-quality restaurant with reasonably priced dishes. **Doubles from €125.**

ONLY YOU HOTEL & LOUNGE > C/Barquillo 21 Ⓜ Chueca ☎ 910 052 222, Ⓦ onlyyouhotels.com. MAP PP.82–83, POCKET MAP G4. A new arrival on the scene, this boutique-style hotel, housed in a refurbished nineteenth-century building, is in a great location between Chueca and Recoletos. There are seventy chic, individually decorated rooms, plus a gastrobar and cocktail bar and a small gym. **Doubles from €150.**

PETIT PALACE DUCAL > C/Hortaleza 3 Ⓜ Gran Vía ☎ 915 211 043, Ⓦ petitpalace.com. MAP PP.82–83, POCKET MAP F4. A former *hostal* upgraded and refurbished to become one of the *Petit Palace* chain of hotels. Situated in the heart of Chueca, it has 58 sleek rooms (including larger family rooms for around €120) with all manner of mod cons. **Doubles around €85.**

ROOM MATE OSCAR > Plaza Vázquez de Mella 12 Ⓜ Gran Vía ☎ 917 011 173, Ⓦ room-matehotels.com. MAP PP.82–83, POCKET MAP F4. Part of the hip *Room Mate* chain, this hotel is in the heart of Chueca and popular with the gay community. It has a garish psychedelic lobby, super cool sparkling white bar area, as well as space age, design-conscious rooms and a rooftop splash pool popular for evening cocktails. **Doubles from €90.**

U HOSTEL MADRID > C/Sagasta 22 Ⓜ Alonso Martínez ☎ 914 450 300, Ⓦ uhostels.com. MAP PP.82–83, POCKET MAP G2. Spacious, comfortable and smart rooms in this sparkling new hostel which sprawls its way over five floors of a renovated building close to the pleasant Plaza Santa Bárbara. Options include en-suite doubles, family suites, quadruples, female dormitories and six-, eight- and twelve-bed dormitories. Other extras include a/c, free wi-fi, a chill-out zone and a €3 breakfast. **Dorm beds from €16.50, doubles from €50.**

Salamanca & Chamberí

HOSTAL RESIDENCIA DON DIEGO > C/Velázquez 45, 5° Ⓜ Velázquez ☎ 914 350 760, Ⓦ hostaldondiego .com. MAP P.92, POCKET MAP K2. Although officially a *hostal*, this comfortable, friendly place situated in an upmarket area of town is more like a hotel. The quiet rooms, with full facilities, a/c and free wi-fi, are reasonably priced for the area. Some English-speaking staff. **Doubles from €68.**

HOTEL ORFILA > C/Orfila 6 Ⓜ Alonso Martínez ☎ 917 027 770, Ⓦ www .hotelorfila.com. MAP P.92, POCKET MAP H2. Transport yourself back in time at this exclusive boutique hotel housed in a beautiful nineteenth-century mansion on a quiet street north of Alonso Martínez. Twelve of the exquisite rooms are suites, there is an elegant terrace for tea and drinks and an upmarket restaurant, too. **Doubles from €225.**

HOTEL SANTO MAURO > C/Zurbano 36 Ⓜ Rubén Darío ☎ 913 196 900, Ⓦ hotelacsantomauro.com. MAP P.92, POCKET MAP H1. This is where the Beckhams first installed themselves when David signed for Real Madrid in 2003 and this former aristocrat's residence has all the luxury and exclusivity you'd expect. Palatial rooms, a restaurant that looks like a gentleman's club, a delightful outdoor terrace and an indoor pool are all part of the package. Doubles from €225.

HOTEL ÚNICO > C/Claudio Cuello 67 Ⓜ Serrano ☎ 917 810 173, Ⓦ unicohotelmadrid.com. MAP P.92, POCKET MAP J2. Luxury 44-room boutique-style hotel in a renovated nineteenth-century mansion. Large rooms, bathrooms with power showers, elegant communal areas and a garden terrace. The restaurant (see p.96) is run by distinguished Catalan chef Ramón Freixa. Doubles from €204.

PETIT PALACE EMBASSY SERRANO > C/Serrano 46 Ⓜ Serrano ☎ 914 313 060, Ⓦ petitpalace.com. MAP P.92, POCKET MAP J2. A four-star member of the sleek *Petit Palace* chain of hotels, close to Plaza Colón and in the middle of the upmarket Salamanca shopping district. The *Embassy* has 75 rooms, including ten family ones for up to four people. Free internet access and flat-screen TVs. Doubles from €130.

Plaza de España

CASÓN DEL TORMES > C/Río 7 Ⓜ Plaza de España ☎ 915 419 746, Ⓦ hotelcasondeltormes.com. MAP P.100, POCKET MAP C4. Welcoming

three-star place in a quiet street next to Plaza de España. The 63 a/c, en-suite rooms are functional but very comfortable and hotel facilities include a bar and breakfast room, and helpful, English-speaking staff. **Doubles from €75.**

HOSTAL BUENOS AIRES > Gran Vía 61, 2° Ⓜ Plaza de España ☎ 915 420 102, Ⓦ hoteleshn.com. MAP P.100, POCKET MAP D4. Twenty-five pleasantly decorated but small rooms with a/c, satellite TV, free wi-fi, modern bathrooms, plus double glazing to keep out much of the noise. Doubles from €55.

HOTEL BE LIVE SANTO DOMINGO > C/San Bernardo 1 Ⓜ Santo Domingo ☎ 915 479 800, Ⓦ hotelsantodomingo .es. MAP P.100, POCKET MAP D4. What with the jungle paintings adorning the car park, the private art collection, the hanging garden and the rooftop swimming pool with views over the city, this hotel is full of surprises. Rooms have tasteful individual decor, large beds and walk-in shower rooms. Doubles from €99.

HOTEL EMPERADOR > Gran Vía 53 Ⓜ Santo Domingo ☎ 915 472 800, Ⓦ emperadorhotel.com. MAP P.100, POCKET MAP D4. The main reason to come here is the stunning rooftop swimming pool with its magnificent views. The hotel itself is geared up for the organized tour market and is rather impersonal, but the rooms are large and well decorated. Doubles from €90.

HOTEL TIROL > C/Marqués de Urquijo 4 Ⓜ Argüelles ☎ 915 481 900, Ⓦ t3tirol.com. MAP P.100, POCKET MAP B1. A good option if you are travelling with young children, the *Tirol* provides family rooms with a double bed and bunks or an adjoining kids' room. There is a play area too and the hotel is close to the Parque del Oeste and the teleférico into Casa de Campo. €140–180 for a family of four. Doubles from €99.

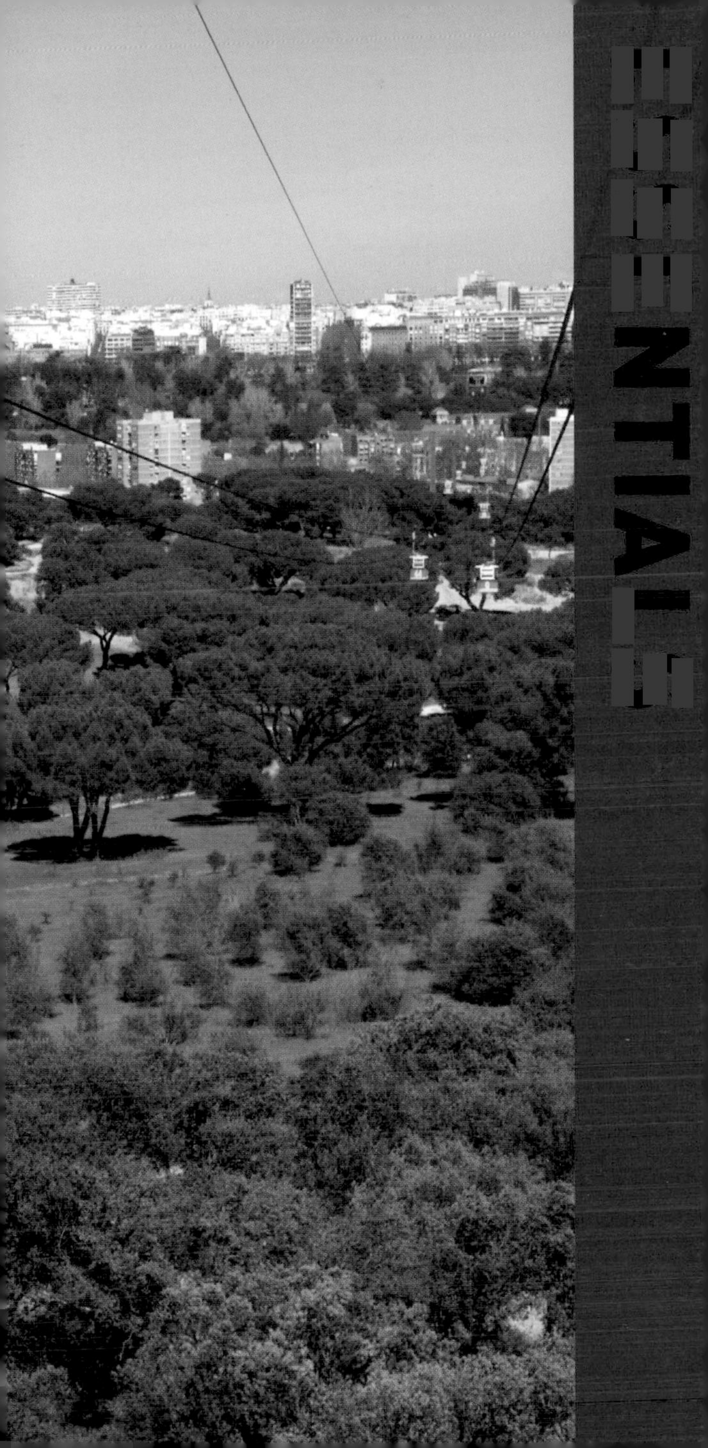

Arrival

Whatever your point of arrival, it's an easy business getting into the centre of Madrid. The airport is connected by metro, shuttle buses and taxis, while the city's main train and bus stations are all linked to the metro system.

By air

The **Aeropuerto Adolfo Suárez Madrid-Barajas** (☎ 913 211 000, ⓦ aena.es) is 16km east of the city. It has four terminals, including the vast T4 building designed by Richard Rogers and Carlos Lamela. All Iberia's domestic and international flights, as well as airlines that belong to the Oneworld group, such as British Airways and American Airlines, use T4 (a 10min shuttle bus ride from the other terminals); other international flights and budget airlines, including Aer Lingus, Easyjet and Ryanair, go from T1, while Air France, KLM and SAS use T2.

From the airport, the **metro link** (Line 8) takes you from T4 and T2 to the city's Nuevos Ministerios station in just twelve minutes (daily 6am–2am; €4.50). From there, connecting metro lines take you to city-centre locations in about fifteen minutes. The new Cercanías train line takes you directly from T4 to Chamartín in the north of the city in twelve minutes (daily 6am–11.30pm; €2.60).

The route by road to central Madrid is more variable, depending on rush-hour traffic, and can take anything from twenty minutes to an hour. Airport express buses run round the clock from each terminal to Cibeles and Atocha (stops only at Cibeles from 11.30pm–6am; every 15–35min; €5) with a journey time of around forty minutes. Taxis are always available outside, too, and cost €30 to the centre (fixed tariff; includes a €5.50 airport supplement).

By train

Trains from France and northern Spain (including the high-speed links to Segovia and Valladolid) arrive at the **Estación de Chamartín**, in the north of the city, connected by metro with the centre, and by regular commuter trains (*trenes de cercanías*) to the more central **Estación de Atocha**. Atocha has two interconnected terminals: one for local services; the other for all points in southern and eastern Spain, including the high-speed services to Barcelona, Seville, Toledo, Malaga, Valencia, Alicante, Albacete and Zaragoza. For train information and **reservations**, call ☎ 902 320 320 or go to ⓦ renfe.com.

By bus

Bus terminals are scattered throughout the city, but the largest – used by all of the international bus services – is the **Estación Sur de Autobuses** at C/Méndez Álvaro 83, 1.5km south of Atocha train station (☎ 914 684 200, ⓦ estaciondeautobuses.com; Ⓜ Méndez Álvaro).

By car

All main roads into Madrid bring you right into the city centre, although eccentric signposting and even more eccentric driving can be unnerving. The two main roads – the M40 and the M30 – and the Paseo de la Castellana, the main north–south artery, are all notorious bottlenecks, although virtually the whole city centre can be close to gridlock during **rush-hour periods** (Mon–Fri 7.30–9.30am & 6–8.30pm). Be prepared for a long trawl around the streets to find **parking** and even when you find somewhere, in most central areas you'll have to buy a ticket at one of the complex roadside meters (€4.80 for a maximum stay of four hours in the blue-coloured bays; €2.35 for a maximum stay of one hour in the green-coloured bays. Charges apply Sept–July Mon–Fri 9am–8pm, Sat 9am–3pm; Aug Mon–Sat 9am–3pm). Another option is to put your car in one of the many signposted parkings (up to €2.50 for an hour and around €31.55 for a day). Once in the city, and with public transport being both efficient and good value, your own vehicle is really only of use for out-of-town excursions.

Getting around

Madrid is an easy city to get around. The central areas are walkable and going on foot is certainly the best way to appreciate and get to know the city. The metro is clean, modern and efficient; buses are also generally very good and serve some of the more out-of-the-way districts, while taxis are always available.

The metro

The **metro** (Ⓦ www.metromadrid .es) is by far the quickest way of getting around Madrid, serving most places you're likely to want to get to. It runs from 6am until 2am and the fare is €1.50–2 for the central zone stations or €12.20 for a ten-trip ticket (*bono de diez viajes*) which can be used on buses too. The network has undergone massive expansion in recent years and some of the outlying commuter districts are now connected by light railways which link with the existing metro stations (supplement fares for some of these). Lines are numbered and colour-coded, and the direction of travel is indicated by the name of the terminus station. You can pick up a free colour map of the system (*plano del metro*) at any station.

Local trains

The **local train** network, or Cercanías, is the most efficient way of connecting between the main train stations and also provides the best route out to many of the suburbs and nearby towns. Most trains are air-conditioned, fares are cheap and there are good connections with the metro. Services generally run

The tourist travel pass

If you're using public transport extensively, it's worth thinking about getting a **tourist pass** (*abono turístico*) covering the metro, train and bus. These are non-transferable and you'll need to show your passport or identity card at the time of purchase. Zone A cards cover the city of Madrid, Zone T cards cover the whole region including Toledo and Guadalajara but not the airport buses. They are available for a duration of one to seven days and range in cost from €8.40 for a Zone A daily card to €70.80 for a weekly one for Zone T (under-11s are half price, under-4s are free) and can be purchased at all metro stations, the airport and tourist offices. If you are staying longer, passes (*abonos*) covering the metro, train and bus are available for a calendar month.

every fifteen to thirty minutes from 6am to around midnight. For more information, go to the RENFE website (w renfe.com) and click on the Cercanías section for Madrid.

Buses

The comprehensive **bus network** (w emtmadrid.es) is a good way to get around and see the sights. There are information booths at Plaza de la Cibeles and Puerta del Sol, which dispense a huge route map (*plano de los transportes de Madrid*) and also sell bus passes. Fares are similar to the metro, at €1.50 a journey, or €12.20 for a ten-trip ticket (*bono de diez viajes*) which can be used on both forms of transport. When you get on the bus, punch your ticket in a machine by the driver. You can also buy tickets from the driver, but try and have the right money.

Services run from 6am to midnight, with *búho* (owl) buses operating through the night on twenty routes around the central area and out to the suburbs: departures are half-hourly midnight–5.30am from Plaza de la Cibeles.

Taxis

Madrid has thousands of reasonably priced taxis that you can wave down on the street – look for white cars with a diagonal red stripe on the side. Seven or eight euros will get you to most places within the centre and, although it's common to round up the fare, you're not expected to tip. The minimum fare is €2.40 (€2.90 on Sun and hols) and supplements (€3–5.50) are charged for baggage, going to the airport, train and bus stations or outside the city limits. To phone for a taxi, call ☎ 915 478 600 (also for wheelchair-friendly cabs), ☎ 914 051 213, ☎ 913 712 131 or ☎ 914 473 232.

Bicycles

Traditionally a nightmare for cyclists, Madrid is trying to become a more bike-friendly city with the introduction of a new bike hire scheme and the extension of cycle paths and lanes in the centre. The scheme, known as BiciMAD (w bicimad.com), allows you to pick up and return an electric-assisted bike at stations scattered all over the city centre (€4 for 2 hours and €4 for each subsequent hour, with a deposit paid by bank card).

Useful bus routes

#2 From west to east: from Argüelles metro station running along C/Princesa, past Plaza de España, along Gran Vía, past Cibeles and out past the Retiro.

#3 From south to north: Puerta de Toledo, through Sol, up towards Gran Vía and then Alonso Martínez and northwards.

#5 From Sol via Cibeles, Colón and the Paseo de la Castellana to Chamartín.

#27 From Embajadores, via Atocha, up the length of the Castellana to Plaza de Castilla.

#33 From Príncipe Pío out via la Puente de Segovia to the Parque de Atracciones and Zoo in Casa de Campo.

#C1 and C2 The Circular bus route takes a broad circuit round the city from Atocha, via Puerta de Toledo, Príncipe Pío, Plaza de España, Moncloa, Cuatro Caminos, Avenida de América and Goya.

City tours

The *turismo* in Plaza Mayor (see p.28) can supply details of guided **English-language walking tours** around the city on the "Descubre Madrid" programme; these cost from €5.90 (info at ⓦ esmadrid.com/visitasguiadas; tickets ☎ 902 221 424). For a **bus tour** of all the major sights, hop on at the stop between the Prado and the *Ritz* hotel; tickets cost €21 (children €10, under-6s free; ⓦ madridcitytour.es) and allow you to jump on and off at various points throughout the city. Pick-up points include Puerta del Sol, Plaza de Colón, Plaza de España and the Palacio Real. For the more adventurous, Madsegs offers a three-hour **segway tour** of the city (April–Oct 10am, Nov–March noon; meeting point in Plaza de España; €65 plus €15 deposit; ☎ 659 824 499, ⓦ madsegs.com), while GoCar (C/Ferraz 26, near Plaza de España; prices start at €35/hr for a two-person car, all day €99; ☎ 915 594 535, ⓦ gocartours.es/madrid) offers tours in little yellow computer-guided storytelling vehicles. Foodies should try the Madrid Food Tour to explore the city's culinary highlights (from €65; ☎ 695 111 832, ⓦ madridfoodtour.com).

Be aware that it is compulsory for under-16s to wear helmets and that the cycle lanes are also used by cars, though they are supposed to adjust their speed to that of the bicycles.

For bike tours in and around Madrid, get in touch with ⓦ bravobike.com at Juan Alvarez Mendizábal 19 (☎ 915 582 945 or ☎ 607 448 440; ⓜ Ventura Rodríguez) or ⓦ bikespain.info at Plaza de la Villa 1 (☎ 917 590 653; ⓜ Ópera).

Car rental

See p.132 for more information on driving in Madrid. Major operators have branches at the airport and train stations. Central offices include: Avis, Gran Vía 60 (ⓜ Santo Domingo) ☎ 915 484 204, reservations ☎ 902 180 854, ⓦ www.avisworld.com; Enterprise, Atocha ☎ 915 061 846, ⓦ enterprise.es; Europcar, C/San Leonardo 8 (ⓜ Plaza España) ☎ 915 418 892, ⓦ europcar.com; Hertz, Atocha station ☎ 902 023 932, ⓦ hertz.com; EasyCar, ⓦ easycar .com; Pepecar, near to Atocha and Chamartín stations ☎ 807 414 243, ⓦ pepecar.com.

Directory A-Z

Addresses

Calle (street) is abbreviated to C/ in addresses, followed by the number on the street, then another number that indicates the floor, eg C/Arenal 23, 5° means fifth floor of no. 23 Arenal Street. You may also see *izquierda* and *derecha*, meaning (apartment or office) left or right of the staircase.

Cinema

Madrileños love going to the cinema (*cine*) and, though most foreign films are dubbed into Spanish, a number of cinemas have original-language screenings, listed in a separate *subtitulada/versión original* (v.o.) section in the newspapers. Tickets cost around €9 but most cinemas have a *día del espectador* (usually Mon or Wed) with a reduced admission charge. Be warned that on Sunday night what seems like

For the police, medical services and the fire brigade, call ☎ 112.

half of Madrid goes to the movies and queues can be long. The most central cinemas showing v.o. films include the two Renoirs at C/Martín de los Heros 12 and C/Princesa 5, and Golem at C/Martín de los Heros 14, all next to Plaza de España, and the nine-screen Ideal Yelmo Complex, C/Doctor Cortezo 6, south off C/Atocha and near Plaza Santa Ana (Ⓜ Sol).

Crime

Central Madrid is so densely populated – and so busy at just about every hour of the day and night – that it seems to carry very little "big city" threat. However, that's not to say that crime is not a problem, nor that there aren't any sleazy areas to be avoided. Tourists in Madrid, as everywhere, are prime targets for pickpockets and petty thieves so take care of belongings in crowded areas, on buses, in the metro, burger bars and in the Rastro. Be aware also that although the city council has taken steps to combat the problem, the main routes through Casa de Campo and the Parque del Oeste are still frequented by prostitutes and are best steered clear of at night. Calle Montera, near Sol, and some streets just north of Gran Vía are also affected.

Electricity

220 volts. Plugs are two round pins.

Embassies and consulates

Australia, Torre Espacio, Paseo de la Castellana 259D (☎ 913 536 600, ⓦ spain.embassy.gov.au; Ⓜ Begoña); Britain, Torre Espacio, Paseo de la Castellana 259D (☎ 917 146 300 or ☎ 902 109 356, ⓦ www.gov.uk /government/world/spain; Ⓜ Begoña); Canada, Torre Espacio, Paseo de la Castellana 259D (☎ 913 828 400, ⓦ canadainternational.gc.ca);

Ⓜ Begoña); Ireland, Paseo de la Castellana 46 (☎ 914 364 093, ⓦ dfa.ie/irish-embassy/spain; Ⓜ Rubén Darío); New Zealand, C/Pinar 7, 3° (☎ 915 230 226, ⓦ nzembassy .com/spain; Ⓜ Gregorio Marañon); US, C/Serrano 75 (☎ 915 872 200, ⓦ spanish.madrid.usembassy.gov; Ⓜ Rubén Darío); South Africa, C/Claudio Coello 91 (☎ 914 363 780, ⓦ www.dirco.gov.za/madrid; Ⓜ Rubén Darío).

Gay and lesbian travellers

The main gay organization in Madrid is Coordinadora Gay de Madrid, C/Puebla 9 (Mon–Fri 10am–2pm & 5–8pm; ☎ 915 230 070, ⓦ www .cogam.org; Ⓜ Gran Vía), which can give information on health, leisure and gay rights. Feminist and lesbian groups are based at the Centro de la Mujer, C/Barquillo 44, 1° izda (☎ 913 081 233; Ⓜ Chueca). For a good one-stop shop with lots of info on the gay scene, try Berkana Bookshop, C/Hortaleza 62 (Mon–Sat 10.30am–9pm, Sun noon–2pm & 5–9pm; ⓦ libreriaberkana.com; Ⓜ Chueca).

Health

Health centres are scattered throughout the city and open 24 hours: one of the most central is at Carrera San Jerónimo 32 (☎ 913 690 491; Ⓜ Sol). Central hospitals include El Clínico San Carlos, C/Profesor Martín Lagos s/n (☎ 913 303 000; Ⓜ Islas Filipinas); Hospital Gregorio Marañon, C/Dr Esquerdo 46 (☎ 915 868 000; Ⓜ O'Donnell); Ciudad Sanitaria La Paz, Paseo de la Castellana 261 (☎ 917 277 000, Ⓜ Begoña). English-speaking doctors are available at the Anglo-American Medical Unit, C/Conde de Aranda 1 (☎ 914 351 823; Mon–Fri 9am–8pm, Sat 10am–3pm; Ⓜ Retiro). The

Clinica Dental Plaza Prosperidad at Plaza Prosperidad 3, 2ºB (📞 914 158 197, 🌐 clinicadentalplazaprosperidad.com; Ⓜ Prosperidad) has some English-speaking dentists as does the Clinica Dental Cisne at C/Magallanes 18 (📞 914 463 221, 🌐 cisnedental.com; Ⓜ Quevedo). The following **pharmacies** (distinguished by a green cross) are open 24 hours: C/Mayor 59 (📞 915 480 014; Ⓜ Sol); C/Toledo 46 (📞 913 653 458; Ⓜ La Latina); C/Atocha 46 (📞 913 692 000; Ⓜ Antón Martín); C/Goya 12 (📞 915 754 924; Ⓜ Serrano).

Internet

There are free wi-fi hotspots at many newspaper stands in the city and on buses, while the city centre is peppered with *locutorios* that provide internet, and most hotels have free wi-fi. *Café Comercial* on the Glorieta de Bilbao has an internet café upstairs. Prices range from €1 to €3.50 per hour.

Left luggage

There are left-luggage facilties (*consignas*) at Barajas Airport in terminals 1, 2 and 4 (open 24hr; €10/day); the Estación Sur bus station; and lockers at Atocha (open 5.30am–10.15pm; €3–5.20/day) and Chamartín (open 7am–11pm; €3–5.20/day) train stations.

Lost property

For lost property, ring the municipal depot on 📞 915 279 590 at Paseo del Molino 7 (open Mon–Fri 9am–2pm; Ⓜ Legazpi); bring ID. For property left in a taxi, call 📞 914 804 613; on a bus, call 📞 902 507 850; on the metro, call 📞 917 212 957.

Money

Banks are plentiful throughout the city and are the best places to change money. Opening hours are normally Mon–Fri 8.30am–2pm. Branches of El Corte Inglés have exchange offices with long hours and reasonably competitive rates; the most central is on C/Preciados, close to Puerta del Sol. Barajas Airport also has a 24 hour currency exchange office. The rates at the exchange bureaux scattered around the city are often very poor, though they don't usually charge commission. ATM cash machines (*cajeros automáticos*) are widespread and accept most credit and debit cards. Credit cards are widely accepted in hotels, restaurants and shops.

Opening hours

Smaller shops generally open 10am–2pm and 5–8pm Mon–Fri, but only open in the mornings on Sat. Department stores and chains tend not to close for lunch and open all day Sat; larger ones open on the first Sun of the month too (except in Aug). Stores in the tourist zones in the centre also open on Sun. Restaurants generally serve from 1.30–4pm and 8.30pm–11.30pm, with many closing for a rest day on Mon. Bars stay open till the early hours – usually around 2am – while clubs close around 5am, depending on the licence they hold. Museums close on Jan 1, Jan 6, May 1, Dec 24 and 31.

Phones

International calls can be made from any phone box or *locutorio* (call centre). The latter are plentiful in the centre and often cheaper than phone boxes. Calling Madrid from abroad, dial your international access code, then 34, followed by the subscriber's number which will nearly always start with 91. Mobile phone users from the UK should be able to use their phones in Spain – check with your service provider before leaving about costs. Many American cellphones do not work with the Spanish mobile network. For national directory enquiries, ring ☎ 11818; for international enquiries, call ☎ 11825.

Post offices

Centrally located post offices are at Paseo del Prado 1 and in El Corte Inglés, C/Preciados 3 (Ⓜ Sol) and there's another with extended hours at C/Mejía Lequerica 7 (Ⓜ Alonso Martínez). Buy stamps (sellos) at estancos.

Public holidays

The main national holidays are: Jan 1 (Año Nuevo); Jan 6 (Reyes); Easter Thursday (Jueves Santo); Good Friday (Viernes Santo); May 1 (Fiesta del Trabajo); May 2 (Día de la Comunidad); May 15 (San Isidro); Aug 15 (Virgen de la Paloma); Oct 12 (Día de la Hispanidad); Nov 1 (Todos Los Santos); Nov 9 (Virgen de la Almudena); Dec 6 (Día de la Constitución); Dec 8 (La Inmaculada); Dec 25 (Navidad).

Smoking

Smoking is banned in all bars, restaurants and clubs, though it is common on outdoor terrazas.

Swimming pools and aquaparks

The Piscina Canal Isabel II, Avda de Filipinas 54 (daily 10am–8.30pm; Ⓜ Ríos Rosas), is a large outdoor swimming pool, and the best central option. Alternatively, try the open-air piscinas at Casa de Campo (daily 10am–8.30pm; Ⓜ Lago) or the Centro Municipal Vicente del Bosque at Avda Monforte de Lemos 13 (10am–8.30pm; Ⓜ Begoña). There are also a number of aquaparks around the city, the closest being Aquópolis de San Fernando (ⓦ san-fernando .aquopolis.es), 16km out on the N-II

Barcelona road (buses #281, #282 and #284 from the intercambiador at Arda de América). Outside May–Sept, most outdoor pools are closed.

Ticket agencies

For theatre and concert tickets, try: Atrapalo ☎ 902 200 808, ⓦ atrapalo .com; ⓦ entradas.com; El Corte Inglés ☎ 902 400 222, ⓦ elcorteingles.es; FNAC ☎ 915 956 100, ⓦ fnac.es; and Ticketmaster ⓦ ticketmaster.es.

Time

Madrid is one hour ahead of Greenwich Mean Time during winter and two hours ahead from March–Oct. Clocks go forward in late March and back an hour in late Oct.

Tipping

When tipping, adding around five to ten percent to a restaurant bill is acceptable but rarely more than €5, while in bars and taxis, rounding up to the nearest euro is the norm.

Tourist information and passes

The chief tourist offices are at the following locations: Barajas International Airport T1, T2 & T4; T1 (Mon–Sat 8am–8pm, Sun 9am–2pm; ☎ 913 058 656); T2 (daily 9am-8pm; ☎ 914 544 410); T4 (daily 9am–8pm; ☎ 913 338 248); Colón (daily 9.30am–8.30pm; ☎ 915 881 636; Ⓜ Colón), in the underground passageway accessed at the corner of C/Goya; Palacio de Cibeles (Tues–Sun 8am–8pm; Ⓜ Banco de España); Estación de Atocha (Mon–Fri 9am–8pm, Sat & Sun 9am–1pm; ☎ 913 159 976; Ⓜ Atocha Renfe); Estación de Chamartín (Mon–Fri 8am–8pm, Sat 9am–2pm; ☎ 913 159 976; Ⓜ Chamartín); Plaza Mayor 27 (daily 9.30am–8.30pm; ☎ 915 881 636; Ⓜ Sol). These are supplemented by booths near the Prado, the Reina

Sofia and in Plaza del Callao off Gran Vía (daily 9.30am–8.30pm). The Madrid tourist board has a comprehensive website at ⓦesmadrid .com, while the regional one has one covering the whole of the province at ⓦturismomadrid.es. You can phone for tourist information in English on ☏ 902 100 007, a premium-rate number that links all the regional tourist offices mentioned below, and on ☏ 914 544 410.

Listings information is in plentiful supply in Madrid. The newspapers *El País* (ⓦelpais.es) and *El Mundo* (ⓦmetropoli.com) have excellent daily listings (in Spanish), and on Friday both publish magazine sections devoted to events, bars and restaurants. The *ayuntamiento* (city council) also publishes a monthly what's-on magazine, *esMadrid* (in English and Spanish), free from any of the tourist offices. Finally, ⓦnakedmadrid.com is an English-language website that features useful reviews of bars and restaurants.

The Madrid **tourist card** (☏902 877 996, ⓦmadridcard.com) gives the holder admission to over fifty museums and sights, a tour of the Bernabéu, the teleférico, a guided walk of the old city, plus discounts at some shops and restaurants. It costs €47 for one day (€60 for two, €67 for three) and is on sale online. It can be collected from offices at C/Mayor 42 (daily 9am–7pm) or at the I-Neo offices in Barajas International Airport T2 & T4 (Mon–Sat 8am–8pm, Sun 8.30am–4.30pm). Do your sums before you splash out though, as you need to cram a lot into a day's sightseeing to get your money's worth and if you want to concentrate on the big three art galleries, the Paseo del Arte ticket (see p.70) is better value.

Theatre

Madrid has a vibrant theatre scene which, if you speak the language, is worth sampling. You can catch anything from Lope de Vega to contemporary productions, and there's a good range on offer during the annual Festival de Otoño a Primavera (Oct–June). For current productions, check the listings sources above.

Travelling with children

Although many of Madrid's main sights may lack children-specific activities, there's still plenty to keep kids occupied during a short stay, from various parks – including the Retiro (see p.72) – to swimming pools (see opposite) and the zoo (see p.104). There is also an ecological theme park/zoo on the outskirts of the city (ⓦfaunia.es). Children are doted on in Spain and welcome in nearly all cafés and restaurants.

Travellers with disabilities

Madrid is slowly getting geared up for disabled visitors (*minusválidos*). The local authority has produced a guide with some practical advice at ⓦesmadrid.com/en/accessible -madrid. The Organizacíon Nacional de Ciegos de España (ONCE; National Organization for the Blind, C/Prim 3 (☏915 325 000, ⓦwww.once.es; ⓜChueca) provides specialist advice, as does the Federación de Asociaciones de Minusválidos Físicos de la Comunidad de Madrid (FAMMA) at C/Galileo 69 (☏915 933 550, ⓦfamma.org; ⓜIslas Filipinas). ⓦdiscapnet.es is a useful source of information (Spanish only). Wheelchair-accessible taxis can be ordered from Eurotaxi (☏630 026 478 or 687 924 027) and Radio Taxi (☏915 478 200 or 915 478 600).

Festivals and events

As well as these festivals, check out the **cultural events** organized by the city council, in particular the Veranos de la Villa (July–Sept) and Festival de Otoño a Primavera (Oct–June), which include music concerts, theatre and cinema. There are annual festivals for flamenco (June), books (end of May), dance (Nov), photography (mid-June to mid-July) and jazz (Nov). See ⓦ esmadrid.com.

CABALGATA DE LOS REYES

January 5
To celebrate the arrival of the gift-bearing Three Kings, there is a gigantic, hugely popular evening procession through the city centre in which children are showered with sweets. It's held on the evening before presents are traditionally exchanged in Spain.

CARNAVAL

The week before Lent
Partying and fancy-dress parades, especially in the gay zone around Chueca. The end of Carnaval is marked by the bizarre parade, El Entierro de la Sardina (The Burial of the Sardine), on Paseo de la Florida.

SEMANA SANTA

Easter week is celebrated with a series of solemn processions around Madrid, with Jueves Santo (Maundy Thursday) and Viernes Santo (Good Friday) both public holidays in the city.

FIESTA DEL DOS DE MAYO

May 2
Celebrations are held around Madrid to commemorate the city's uprising against the French in 1808.

FIESTAS DE SAN ISIDRO

May 15, for a week.
Evenings start out with traditional chotis, music and dancing, and bands play each night in the Jardines de las Vistillas (south of the Palacio Real). The fiestas mark the start of the bullfighting season.

LA FERIA DEL LIBRO

End of May
Madrid's great book fair takes place with stands set up in the Retiro Park.

GAY PRIDE WEEK

End of June or beginning of July
Gay Pride is a week-long party in Chueca culminating in a parade that brings the city centre to a standstill.

CASTIZO FIESTAS

August 6 to 15
Madrileños put on traditional fiestas to celebrate the saints' days of San Cayetano, San Lorenzo and La Virgen de la Paloma. Much of the activity centres around C/Toledo, Plaza de la Paja and the Jardines de las Vistillas.

NAVIDAD

The Christmas period in Madrid sees Plaza Mayor taken over by a model of a Nativity crib and a large seasonal market with stalls selling all manner of festive decorations.

NOCHE VIEJA

Dec 31
Puerta del Sol is the customary place to gather for midnight, waiting for the strokes of the clock and then attempting to swallow a grape on each strike to bring good luck in the coming year.

Chronology

800s > Muslims establish a defensive outpost on the escarpment above the Manzanares river. It becomes known as "mayrit" – the place of many springs – successively modified to Magerit and then Madrid.

1086 > Madrid taken by the Christians under Alfonso VI, but it remains a relatively insignificant backwater.

1561 > Felipe II chooses Madrid as a permanent home for the court because of its position in the centre of the recently unified Spain. The population surges with the arrival of the royal entourage, and there is a boom in the building industry.

1700–46 > With the emergence of the Bourbon dynasty under Felipe V, a touch of French style, including the sumptuous Palacio Real, is introduced into the capital.

1759–88 > Carlos III tries to make the city into a home worthy of the monarchy. Streets are cleaned up, sewers and street lighting installed, and work begins on the Museo del Prado.

1795–1808 > Spain falls under the influence of Napoleonic France, with their troops entering the capital in 1808. The heavily out-gunned *Madrileños* are defeated in a rising on May 2 and Napoleon installs his brother Joseph on the throne.

1812–14 > The French are removed by a combined Spanish and British army and the monarchy makes a return under the reactionary Fernando VII.

1833–75 > Spanish society is riven with divisions which explode into a series of conflicts known as the Carlist Wars and lead to chronic political instability, including a brief period as a republic.

1875–1900 > Madrid undergoes significant social changes prompted by a rapid growth in population and the emergence of a working class. The socialist party, the PSOE, is founded in the city in 1879.

1923–31 > A hard-line military regime under Miguel Primo de Rivera takes control, with King Alfonso XIII relegated to the background. The king eventually decides to abdicate in 1931, and the Second Republic is ushered in.

1936–39 > The Right grows increasingly restless and a group of army generals organize an uprising in July 1936 which ignites the Spanish Civil War. Madrid resists and becomes a Republican stronghold.

1939 > Franco and his victorious Nationalists enter the city. Mass reprisals take place and Franco installs himself in the country residence of El Pardo.

1939–53 > Spain endures yet more suffering during the post-war years until a turnaround in American policy. The Pact of Madrid is signed to rehabilitate Franco, as the US searches for anti-Communist Cold War allies.

1970s > Franco eventually dies in November 1975. He is succeeded by King Juan Carlos who presides over the transition to democracy.

1981 > In a last-gasp attempt to re-establish itself, the military under Colonel Tejero storms the parliament in Madrid, but a lack of support from the king and army cause its collapse. The Socialists led by Felipe González win the 1982 elections.

1980s > Freedom from the shackles of dictatorship and the release of long-pent-up creative forces help create *La Movida*, with Madrid becoming the epicentre of the movement.

1990s > The Socialists become increasingly discredited as they are entangled in a web of scandal and corruption, losing control of Madrid in 1991 and the country in 1996 to the conservative Partido Popular (PP).

1992 > Madrid was named European Capital of Culture.

2004 > The March 11 bombings carried out by Muslim extremists at Atocha train station kill 191 and injure close to 2000. The Socialists return to power in the general elections which follow, although the PP remain firmly in control of the local government.

2004–08 > Madrid fails in its bids for the 2012 and 2016 Olympics, losing out to London and then Rio de Janeiro. High-profile building projects such as the Richard Rogers airport terminal, Norman Foster's Torre Caja Madrid skyscraper, Rafael Moneo's Prado extension and the M30 ring road 6-km long mega-tunnel are all completed before the onset of the recession and the end of the property boom.

2008–13 > The effects of the global economic crisis combined with the endemic problems of property speculation, profligate spending on showcase projects and corruption mean the crisis hits Spain even harder. The centre-right Popular Party is returned to power in the 2011 general election. Unemployment reaches record highs, the economy flatlines in terms of growth and corruption scandals continue to plague the country.

2014 > Juan Carlos abdicates after nearly forty years on the throne. His son Felipe succeeds as King of Spain.

Spanish

Once you get into it, Spanish is one of the easiest languages around, and people are eager to try and understand even the most faltering attempt. English is spoken at the main tourist attractions, but you'll get a far better reception if you try communicating with *Madrileños* in their own tongue.

Pronunciation

The rules of pronunciation are pretty straightforward and strictly observed.

A somewhere between the A sound of back and that of father.

E as in get.

I as in police.

O as in hot.

U as in rule.

C is spoken like a TH before E and I, hard otherwise: *cerca* is pronounced "thairka".

G is a guttural H sound (like the ch in loch) before E or I, a hard G elsewhere – *gigante* becomes "higante".

H is always silent.

J is the same as a guttural G: *jamón* is "hamon".

LL sounds like an English Y: *tortilla* is pronounced "torteeya".

N is as in English unless it has a tilde (accent) over it, when it becomes NY: *mañana* sounds like "manyana".

QU is pronounced like an English K.

R is rolled when it is at the start of a word, RR doubly so.

V sounds more like B, *vino* becoming "beano".

X has an S sound before consonants, normal X before vowels.

Z is the same as a soft C, so *cerveza* becomes "thairbaytha".

Words and phrases

BASICS

yes, no, ok	sí, no, vale
please, thank you	por favor, gracias
where?, when?	¿dónde?, ¿cuándo?
what?, how much?	¿qué?, ¿cuánto?
here, there	aquí, allí
this, that	esto, eso
now, later	ahora, más tarde
open, closed	abierto/a, cerrado/a
with, without	con, sin
good, bad	buen(o)/a, mal(o)/a
big, small	gran(de), pequeño/a
cheap, expensive	barato, caro
hot, cold	caliente, frío
more, less	más, menos
today, tomorrow	hoy, mañana
yesterday	ayer
the bill	la cuenta
price	precio
free	gratis

GREETINGS AND RESPONSES

hello, goodbye	hola, adiós
good morning	buenos días
good afternoon/ night	buenas tardes/ noches
see you later	hasta luego
sorry	lo siento/disculpe
excuse me	con permiso/perdón
How are you?	¿Cómo está (usted)?
I (don't) understand	(no) entiendo
not at all/you're welcome	de nada
Do you speak english?	¿Habla (usted) inglés?
I (don't) speak Spanish	(no) hablo español
My name is...	Me llamo...
What's your name?	¿Cómo se llama usted?
I am English/ Scottish/ Welsh/ Australian/ Canadian/ American/ Irish/ New Zealander	Soy inglés(a)/ escocés(a)/ galés(a)/ australiano(a)/ canadiense/ americano(a)/ irlandés(a)/ neozelandés(a)

HOTELS, TRANSPORT AND DIRECTIONS

I want	Quiero
I'd like	Quisiera
Do you know...?	¿Sabe....?

English	Spanish
I don't know	No sé
Give me (one like that)	Deme (uno así)
Do you have...?	¿Tiene...?
the time	la hora
two beds/double bed	dos camas/cama matrimonial
with shower/bath	con ducha/baño
it's for one person	es para una persona
for one night	para una noche
for one week	para una semana
How do I get to...?	¿Por dónde se va a....?
left, right, straight on	izquierda, derecha, todo recto
Where is the bus station/post office/toilet?	¿Dónde está la estación de autobuses/la oficina de correos/el baño?
What´s this in Spanish?	¿Cómo se dice en español?
Where does the bus to... leave from?	¿De dónde sale el autobús para...?
I'd like a (return) ticket to...	Quisiera un billete (de ida y vuelta) para...
What time does it leave?	¿A qué hora sale?

MONEY

How much?	¿Cuánto es?
I would like to change some money	Me gustaría cambiar dinero
ATM cash machine	cajero automático
foreign exchange bureau	la oficina de cambio
credit card	tarjeta de crédito
travellers' cheques	cheques de viaje

NUMBERS/DAYS/MONTHS/SEASONS

1	un/uno/una
2	dos
3	tres
4	cuatro
5	cinco
6	seis
7	siete
8	ocho
9	nueve
10	diez
11	once
12	doce
13	trece
14	catorce
15	quince
16	dieciséis
17	diecisiete
18	dieciocho
19	diecinueve
20	veinte
21	veintiuno
30	treinta
40	cuarenta
50	cincuenta
60	sesenta
70	setenta
80	ochenta
90	noventa
100	cien(to)
101	ciento uno
200	doscientos
500	quinientos
1000	mil
Monday	lunes
Tuesday	martes
Wednesday	miércoles
Thursday	jueves
Friday	viernes
Saturday	sábado
Sunday	domingo
today	hoy
yesterday	ayer
tomorrow	mañana
January	enero
February	febrero
March	marzo
April	abril
May	mayo
June	junio
July	julio
August	agosto
September	septiembre
October	octubre
November	noviembre
December	diciembre
spring	primavera
summer	verano
autumn	otoño
winter	invierno

Food and drink

BASICS

aceite	oil
agua	water
ajo	garlic
arroz	rice
azúcar	sugar
huevos	eggs
mantequilla	butter
miel	honey
pan	bread
pimienta	pepper
pinchos/pintxos	a small bite-sized tapa
queso	cheese
sal	salt
sopa	soup
tapa	small serving of food
vinagre	vinegar

MEALS

almuerzo/comida	lunch
botella	bottle
carta	menu
cena	dinner
comedor	dining room
cuchara	spoon
cuchillo	knife
desayuno	breakfast
menú (del día)	daily set-lunch
menú de degustación	set menu offering a taste of several house specialities
mesa	table
platos combinados	mixed plate
ración	a plateful of food
tenedor	fork
vaso	glass

MEAT

albóndigas	meatballs
callos	tripe
caracoles	snails
chorizo	spicy sausage
conejo	rabbit
cochinillo	roast suckling pig
hígado	liver
jamón serrano	cured ham
jamón de york	regular ham
morcilla	black pudding
pollo	chicken
salchicha	sausage

SEAFOOD

ahumados	smoked fish
almejas	clams
anchoas	anchovies
atún	tuna
a la marinera	seafood cooked with garlic, onions and white wine
bacalao	cod
bonito	tuna
boquerones	small, anchovy-like fish, usually served in vinegar
calamares	squid
cangrejo	crab
champiñones	mushrooms
gambas	prawns
langostinos	langoustines
mejillones	mussels
ostras	oysters
pulpo	octopus

FRUIT AND VEGETABLES

aceitunas	olives
alcachofas	artichokes
berenjena	aubergine/eggplant
cebolla	onion
cerezas	cherries
coliflor	cauliflower
ensalada	salad
fresa	strawberry
granada	pomegranate
habas	broad/fava beans
higos	figs
lechuga	lettuce
lentejas	lentils
limón	lemon
manzana	apple
melocotones	peaches
nabos	turnips
naranja	orange
pepino	cucumber
pimientos	peppers

pimientos de padrón	small peppers, with the odd hot one thrown in
piña	pineapple
pisto	assortment of cooked vegetables (like ratatouille)
plátano	banana
pomelo	grapefruit
puerros	leeks
puré	thick soup
repollo	cabbage
sandía	watermelon
setas	oyster mushrooms
tomate	tomato
uvas	grapes
zanahoria	carrot

SPECIALITIES

bocadillo	French-loaf sandwich
cocido	meat and chickpea stew
croquetas	croquettes, with bits of ham in
empanada	slices of fish/ meat pie
ensaladilla	Russian salad (diced vegetables in mayonnaise, often with tuna)
patatas alioli	potatoes in garlic mayonnaise
patatas bravas	fried potatoes in spicy tomato sauce
tortilla (española)	potato omelette
tortilla francesa	plain omelette
tostas	toasted bread with a topping

COOKING METHODS

al ajillo	with olive oil and garlic
a la parilla	charcoal-grilled
a la plancha	grilled on a hot plate
a la romana	fried in batter
al horno	baked in the oven
asado	roast
frito	fried

DESSERTS

arroz con leche	rice pudding
crema catalana	Catalan crème brûlée
cuajada	cream-based dessert often served with honey
flan	crème caramel
helado	ice cream
melocotón en almíbar	peaches in syrup
membrillo	quince paste
nata	whipped cream
natillas	custard
yogur	yoghurt

DRINKS

anís	aniseed liqueur
café (con leche)	(white) coffee
cerveza	beer
té	tea
vino	wine
...blanco	white
...rosado	rosé
...tinto	red
vermút	vermouth
zumo	juice

Glossary

alameda park or grassy promenade

alcázar Moorish fortified palace

avenida avenue (usually abbreviated to avda)

ayuntamiento town hall or council

azulejo glazed ceramic tilework

barrio suburb or neighbourhood

bodega cellar or wine bar

calle (usually abbreviated to C/) street or road

capilla mayor chapel containing the high altar

capilla real royal chapel

castillo castle

cervecería bar specializing in beers

correos post office

corrida bullfight

cuadrilla a bullfighter's team of assistants

edificio building

ermita hermitage

estanco small shop selling stamps and tobacco, recognizable by the brown and yellow signs bearing the word *tabacos*

iglesia church

lonja stock exchange building

marisquería seafood restaurant

mercado market

mesón an old-style restaurant

mirador viewing point

Movida late Seventies/early Eighties creative explosion in Madrid, viewed as Spain's Swinging Sixties

Mudéjar Muslim Spaniard subject to medieval Christian rule, but retaining Islamic worship; most commonly a term applied to architecture which includes buildings built by Moorish craftsmen for the Christian rulers and later designs influenced by Moors. The 1890s to 1930s saw a Mudéjar revival, blended with Art Nouveau and Art Deco forms

museo museum

palacio aristocratic mansion

parador state-run hotel, usually housed in a building of historic interest

patio inner courtyard

Plateresque elaborately decorative Renaissance style, the sixteenth-century successor of Isabelline forms. Named for its resemblance to silversmiths' work (plateria)

plaza square

plaza de toros bullring

posada old name for an inn

puerta gateway

puerto port

sidrería bar specializing in cider

terraza summer outdoor bar

oficina de turismo tourist office

zarzuela light opera

PUBLISHING INFORMATION

This third edition published January 2016 by **Rough Guides Ltd**

80 Strand, London WC2R 0RL

11, Community Centre, Panchsheel Park, New Delhi 110017, India

Distributed by Penguin Random House

Penguin Books Ltd, 80 Strand, London WC2R 0RL

Penguin Group (USA) 345 Hudson Street, NY 10014, USA

Penguin Group (Australia) 250 Camberwell Road, Camberwell, Victoria 3124, Australia

Penguin Group (NZ) 67 Apollo Drive, Mairangi Bay, Auckland 1310, New Zealand

Penguin Group (South Africa) Block D, Rosebank Office Park, 181 Jan Smuts Avenue,
Parktown North, Gauteng, South Africa 2193

Rough Guides is represented in Canada by

Tourmaline Editions Inc., 662 King Street West, Suite 304, Toronto, Ontario, M5V 1M7

Typeset in Minion and Din to an original design by Henry Iles and Dan May.

Printed and bound in China

© Simon Baskett 2016

Maps © Rough Guides except Madrid Metro map © Metro de Madrid S.A. 2015

160pp includes index

A catalogue record for this book is available from the British Library

ISBN 978-0-24120-422-1

The publishers and authors have done their best to ensure the accuracy and currency of all the
information in **Pocket Rough Guide Madrid**, however, they can accept no responsibility for
any loss, injury, or inconvenience sustained by any traveller as a result of information or advice
contained in the guide.

1 3 5 7 9 8 6 4 2

ROUGH GUIDES CREDITS

Editor: Rebecca Hallett

Layout: Nikhil Agarwal

Cartography: Ed Wright

Picture editor: Phoebe Lowndes

Photographers: Lydia Evans, Tim Draper

Proofreader: Norm Longley

Managing editor: Monica Woods

Production: Jimmy Lao

Cover design: Nikhil Agarwal, Nicole Newman

Editorial assistant: Freya Godfrey

Senior pre-press designer: Dan May

Publisher: Keith Drew

Publishing director: Georgina Dee

THE AUTHOR

Simon Baskett lives and works in Madrid with his wife, Trini, and two children Patrick and Laura. He
is a long-suffering Atlético Madrid fan, and has not yet given up hope that he might live long enough
to see them win the Champions League. His ambition is to win El Gordo (the huge Christmas lottery)
and retire to a local bar.

ACKNOWLEDGEMENTS

Special thanks to Trini once again for all her hard work and patience. Thanks, too, go to Antonio and Javier of the *Hostal Gonzalo*, to Itziar Herrán and to the Metro de Madrid.

HELP US UPDATE

We've gone to a lot of effort to ensure that the third edition of the **Pocket Rough Guide Madrid** is accurate and up-to-date. However, things change – places get "discovered", opening hours are notoriously fickle, restaurants and rooms raise prices or lower standards. If you feel we've got it wrong or left something out, we'd like to know, and if you can remember the address, the price, the hours, the phone number, so much the better.

Please send your comments with the subject line "**Pocket Rough Guide Madrid Update**" to mail@roughguides.com. We'll credit all contributions and send a copy of the next edition (or any other Rough Guide if you prefer) for the very best emails.

Find more travel information, connect with fellow travellers and book your trip on Ⓦ roughguides.com

READERS' UPDATES

Thanks to all the readers who have taken the time to write in with comments and suggestions (and apologies if we've inadvertently omitted or misspelt anyone's name):

Harald Oldenziel, Jonathan Sidaway

PHOTO CREDITS

Index

Maps are marked in **bold**.

150

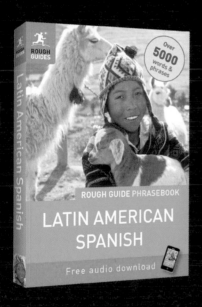

SO NOW WE'VE TOLD YOU
ABOUT THE THINGS NOT TO
MISS, THE BEST PLACES TO
STAY, THE TOP RESTAURANTS,
THE LIVELIEST BARS AND THE
MOST SPECTACULAR SIGHTS,
IT ONLY SEEMS FAIR TO
TELL YOU ABOUT THE BEST
TRAVEL INSURANCE AROUND

WorldNomads.com
keep travelling safely

RECOMMENDED BY ROUGH GUIDES